W9-ALN-494

CHANGING THE CONVERSATION

MESSAGES FOR IMPROVING PUBLIC UNDERSTANDING OF ENGINEERING

Committee on Public Understanding of Engineering Messages

NATIONAL ACADEMY OF ENGINEERING
OF THE NATIONAL ACADEMIES

THE NATIONAL ACADEMIES PRESS
Washington, D.C.
www.nap.edu

NATIONAL ACADEMIES PRESS   500 Fifth Street, N.W.   Washington, DC 20001

NOTICE: This publication has been reviewed according to procedures approved by a National Academy of Engineering report review process. Publication of signed work signifies that it is judged a competent and useful contribution worthy of public consideration, but it does not imply endorsement of conclusions or recommendations by the National Academy of Engineering. The interpretations and conclusions in such publications are those of the authors and do not purport to represent the views of the council, officers, or staff of the National Academy of Engineering.

This study was supported by Contract/Grant No. ENG-0550368 between the National Academy of Sciences and the National Science Foundation and by grants from the Georgia Institute of Technology and S.D. Bechtel, Jr. Foundation. Any opinions, findings, conclusions, or recommendations expressed in this publication are those of the author(s) and do not necessarily reflect the views of the organizations or agencies that provided support for the project.

Library of Congress Cataloging-in-Publication Data

Changing the conversation : messages for improving public understanding of engineering / Committee on Public Understanding of Engineering Messages.
   p. cm.
Includes bibliographical references.
 ISBN 978-0-309-11934-4 (pbk.) — ISBN 978-0-309-11935-1 (pdf) 1.
Engineering—United States. 2. Engineering—Social aspects—United States. 3.
Engineers—United States—Public opinion. I. National Academy of Engineering.
Committee on Public Understanding of Engineering Messages.
 TA160.4.C53 2008
 620.00973—dc22
          2008016992

Copies of this report are available from National Academy Press, 500 Fifth Street, N.W., Lockbox 285, Washington, D.C. 20055; (800) 624-6242 or (202) 334-3313 (in the Washington metropolitan area); online at http://www.nap.edu

Printed in the United States of America

First Printing, May 2008
Second Printing, July 2009

THE NATIONAL ACADEMIES
Advisers to the Nation on Science, Engineering, and Medicine

The **National Academy of Sciences** is a private, nonprofit, self-perpetuating society of distinguished scholars engaged in scientific and engineering research, dedicated to the furtherance of science and technology and to their use for the general welfare. Upon the authority of the charter granted to it by the Congress in 1863, the Academy has a mandate that requires it to advise the federal government on scientific and technical matters. Dr. Ralph J. Cicerone is president of the National Academy of Sciences.

The **National Academy of Engineering** was established in 1964, under the charter of the National Academy of Sciences, as a parallel organization of outstanding engineers. It is autonomous in its administration and in the selection of its members, sharing with the National Academy of Sciences the responsibility for advising the federal government. The National Academy of Engineering also sponsors engineering programs aimed at meeting national needs, encourages education and research, and recognizes the superior achievements of engineers. Dr. Charles M. Vest is president of the National Academy of Engineering.

The **Institute of Medicine** was established in 1970 by the National Academy of Sciences to secure the services of eminent members of appropriate professions in the examination of policy matters pertaining to the health of the public. The Institute acts under the responsibility given to the National Academy of Sciences by its congressional charter to be an adviser to the federal government and, upon its own initiative, to identify issues of medical care, research, and education. Dr. Harvey V. Fineberg is president of the Institute of Medicine.

The **National Research Council** was organized by the National Academy of Sciences in 1916 to associate the broad community of science and technology with the Academy's purposes of furthering knowledge and advising the federal government. Functioning in accordance with general policies determined by the Academy, the Council has become the principal operating agency of both the National Academy of Sciences and the National Academy of Engineering in providing services to the government, the public, and the scientific and engineering communities. The Council is administered jointly by both Academies and the Institute of Medicine. Dr. Ralph J. Cicerone and Dr. Charles M. Vest are chair and vice chair, respectively, of the National Research Council.

www.national-academies.org

COMMITTEE ON PUBLIC UNDERSTANDING OF ENGINEERING MESSAGES

DON P. GIDDENS, *chair,* Georgia Institute of Technology, Atlanta
RICK E. BORCHELT, Johns Hopkins University, Washington, D.C.
VIRGIL R. CARTER, American Society of Mechanical Engineers,
    New York, New York
WILLIAM S. HAMMACK, University of Illinois at Urbana-Champaign
LEAH H. JAMIESON, Purdue University, West Lafayette, Indiana
JAMES H. JOHNSON, JR., Howard University, Washington, D.C.
VIRGINIA KRAMER, Keiler and Company, Farmington, Connecticut
PATRICK J. NATALE, American Society of Civil Engineers, Reston,
    Virginia
DIETRAM A. SCHEUFELE, University of Wisconsin, Madison
JACQUELYN F. SULLIVAN, University of Colorado, Boulder

Project Staff

GREG PEARSON, Study Director and Senior Program Officer,
    National Academy of Engineering
MARIBETH KEITZ, Senior Public Understanding of Engineering
    Associate, National Academy of Engineering
CAROL ARENBERG, Senior Editor, National Academy of
    Engineering
MARIA IVANCIN, *Consultant,* President, Market Research Bureau

PREFACE

This report is the final product of an 18-month study by the Committee on Public Understanding of Engineering Messages, a group of experts on diverse subjects brought together under the auspices of the National Academy of Engineering (NAE). The committee's charge was to identify and test a small number of messages that appear likely to improve the public understanding of engineering. To fulfill that charge, the committee used the services of professional marketing and communications firms, hired through a competitive request-for-proposals process. Working with the committee, these firms conducted qualitative and quantitative research to collect data and develop messages, themes, and taglines based on that data.

This report follows *Raising Public Awareness of Engineering*, an NAE report published in 2002, which revealed that the engineering community has been spending hundreds of millions of dollars annually to promote the public understanding of engineering with little measurable impact on young people or adults. That study's committee concluded that the messages being communicated had not been developed in a systematic way and recommended that more effective, consistent messages be developed and used in a coordinated way by organizations interested in enhancing public understanding of the critical role engineers play in today's world.

Given the concerns in the United States about the importance of STEM (science, technology, engineering, mathematics) education to global competitiveness, national security, and quality of life, the current report is especially timely. But messaging is about much more than "priming" the engineering-education pipeline. The vast majority of Americans will never become engineers, but all Americans—young and old—can benefit by having a better understanding of the role engineers play in the creation of technologies. Effective messaging can help raise the level of technological literacy in the general population, a key competency for the 21st century.

This report will be of special interest to engineering professional societies, technology-intensive industries, colleges of engineering, science and technology centers, and other organizations that communicate with policy makers, K–12 teachers and students, and the public at large about engineering. Federal and state agencies concerned with reforming STEM education and supporting research, innovation, and technology development similarly will find that this report can be useful in outreach efforts.

On behalf of the committee, I urge the engineering community to embrace the very useful information in this document.

Don P. Giddens, *chair*
Committee on Public Understanding
of Engineering Messages

ACKNOWLEDGMENTS

This report has been reviewed, in draft form, by individuals chosen for their diverse perspectives and technical expertise, in accordance with procedures approved by the National Academies. The purpose of this independent review process is to provide candid and critical comments to assist the committee and the National Academy of Engineering (NAE) in making its published reports as sound as possible and to ensure that the report meets institutional standards for objectivity, evidence, and responsiveness to the study charge. The reviewers' comments and the draft manuscript remain confidential to protect the integrity of the deliberative process. We wish to thank the following individuals for their reviews of this report:

Todd R. Allen, Global University Recruitment Team, Johnson & Johnson

Tony Beard, PriceWeber Marketing Communications, Inc.

Leslie Collins, National Engineers Week Foundation

Eugene M. DeLoatch, School of Engineering, Morgan State University

Kimberly D. Douglas, Women in Engineering and Science Program, Kansas State University
Ioannis Miaoulis, Boston Museum of Science
Jon Miller, Department of Political Science, Michigan State University
Teri Reed-Rhoads, College of Engineering, Purdue University
Betty Shanahan, Society of Women Engineers
Lilian Wu, University Relations, IBM

Although the reviewers listed above provided many constructive comments and suggestions, they were not asked to endorse the conclusions or recommendations and did not see the final draft of the report before its public release. The review was overseen by Robert F. Sproull, Sun Microsystems, Inc., who was appointed by NAE to ensure that an independent examination of this report was carried out in accordance with institutional procedures and that all review comments were carefully considered. Responsibility for the final content of this report rests entirely with the authoring committee and NAE.

In addition to the reviewers, the committee wishes to thank consultant Maria Ivancin, Market Research Bureau, who assisted the NAE staff in overseeing the research and provided advice throughout the project. Her input was critical to the success of the study.

The committee also thanks the project staff. Maribeth Keitz managed the committee's logistical and administrative needs, making sure meetings ran efficiently and smoothly. NAE senior editor Carol R. Arenberg substantially improved the readability of the report. Study director Greg Pearson managed the project from start to finish.

CONTENTS

EXECUTIVE SUMMARY   1

1   INTRODUCTION   17
Messages to Promote the Public Understanding of
Engineering, 21
Primer on Market Research: Lexicon and Methods, 23
The NAE Messaging Project, 29

2   DEVELOPMENT OF A POSITIONING STATEMENT,
THEMES, AND MESSAGES   39
Communications Audit, 40
Reframing the Image of Engineering, 44
Developing a Positioning Statement, 45
Conclusion, 49

3   RESEARCH RESULTS   51
Qualitative Research, 52
Quantitative Research, 62
Conclusion, 86

4   CONCLUSIONS AND RECOMMENDATIONS   97
    Using the Positioning Statement, Messages, and Taglines, 98
    Creating a Shared Public-Relations Resource, 102
    Launching a Campaign, 102
    A Final Word, 104

APPENDIXES

A   Biographies of Committee Members   107
B   In-Depth Interviews: Interviewer's Guide   115
C   Focus Groups: Moderator's Guide—Parents   121
D   Focus Groups: Moderator's Guide—Teens   129
E   Youth Triads: Moderator's Guide   135
F   Online Survey   141
G   Complete Data Tables—Online Survey*
    1.   Initial Sample Adults
    2.   Initial Sample Informed Adults
    3.   Initial Sample Teens
    4.   Initial Sample Open-ended Question
    5.   African American Adults Oversample
    6.   African American Teens Oversample
    7.   Hispanic Adults Oversample
    8.   Hispanic Teens Oversample

---

*Appendix G is reproduced on the CD (inside back cover) that contains the full report but is not included in the printed report.

CHANGING THE CONVERSATION

EXECUTIVE SUMMARY

Every year, hundreds of millions of dollars are spent in the United States to improve the public understanding of engineering (NAE, 2002). Despite these efforts, educational research shows that K–12 teachers and students generally have a poor understanding of what engineers do (Cunningham et al., 2005; Cunningham and Knight, 2004). Polling data show that the public believes engineers are not as engaged with societal and community concerns as scientists or as likely to play a role in saving lives (Harris Interactive, 2004). And when asked to judge the relative prestige of professions, people tend to place engineering in the middle of the pack, well below medicine, nursing, science, and teaching (Harris Interactive, 2006). Parents, however, are generally amenable to the idea of their sons and daughters opting for careers in engineering.

Understandably, engineers, engineering educators, and the organizations that represent them want people to have an accurate, more positive impression of engineering. However, there also other important reasons for improving the public understanding of engineering:

- **Sustaining the U.S. capacity for technological innovation.** A better understanding of engineering would educate policy makers and the public as to how engineering contributes to economic development, quality of life, national security, and health.
- **Attracting young people to careers in engineering.** A better understanding of engineering should encourage students to take higher level math and science courses in middle school, thus enabling them to pursue engineering education in the future. This is especially important for girls and underrepresented minorities, who have not historically been attracted to technical careers in large numbers.
- **Improving technological literacy.** To be capable, confident participants in our technology-dependent society, citizens must know something about how engineering and science, among other factors, lead to new technologies (NAE and NRC, 2002).

GOAL OF THE MESSAGING PROJECT

The goal of this project, primarily funded by the National Science Foundation with additional support from the Georgia Institute of Technology and the S.D. Bechtel, Jr. Foundation, is to encourage coordinated, consistent, effective communication by the engineering community to a variety of audiences, including school children, their parents, teachers, and counselors, about the role, importance, and career potential of engineering. The project had three objectives:

- to identify a small number of messages likely to improve the public understanding of engineering
- to test the effectiveness of these messages in a variety of target audiences
- to disseminate the results of the message testing to the engineering community

This project did not have the goal of developing metrics for measuring the effectiveness of messaging efforts. Nevertheless, it is reasonable to ask what one might look for as evidence of "improvement" in public understanding of engineering. One indicator of improvement would be the number and diversity of organizations using this report to shape their engineering outreach. Over time, we would hope to see growth in this set of organizations, and that might be measured through surveys of the engineering community. A longitudinal study, combined with "dipstick" surveys before, during, and after the deployment of new messages, could indicate the extent to which the public recognizes the new messages or associates certain key words, such as creativity and innovation, with engineering.

The remainder of the Executive Summary is focused on survey results for the messages, and it briefly discusses testing data related to several shorter, more punchy "taglines." Additional findings are described in the full report, and complete data tables of the survey results are provided in an accompanying CD. The CD also contains a copy of the full report as a PDF.

METHODOLOGY

Through a request-for-proposals process, the committee selected the communications firm Bemporad Baranowski Marketing Group to oversee message development, in partnership with Global Strategy Group (GSG), a market research company. GSG and Harris Interactive, another market-research firm, were selected to test the messages.

The study used qualitative and quantitative research. The qualitative research included in-depth interviews, youth "triads" (same-sex groups of three 9–11-year-olds), and adult and teen focus groups to determine perceptions of engineers and engineering by different groups as a basis for developing a positioning statement, messages, and taglines. The quantitative research consisted of an online survey that oversampled for African Americans and Hispanics. The goal of the quantitative research was to shed light on the findings of the focus groups and provide a statistically sound foundation for the committee's recommendations. The committee also solicited feedback through presentations at relevant meetings and by posting an interim status report on the National Academy of Engineering (NAE) website to encourage input from a cross section of the engineering community and others.

In the interviews, focus groups, and youth triads, small samples were selected without statistical procedures. The results of this qualitative research had to be tested through quantitative methods. In the quantitative research, the online survey, respondents were part of volunteer survey panels. Thus we could not control exactly who would take part in the survey, and the responses may not accurately reflect the demographics of the sample populations. This common limitation was addressed by weighting (i.e., adjusting survey responses upward or downward to match the demographic variable of interest). Nonresponses also affect the representativeness of a sample, and thus the "generalizability" of the results. Another limitation was that respondents were required to have access to the Internet. In the committee's view, these methodological issues do not detract from the usefulness of the study's findings.

THE ENGINEERING MESSAGING LANDSCAPE

Current and past engineering outreach to the public and message development have been ad hoc efforts, and metrics for tracking results have rarely been used. Although a variety of useful tactics have been tried, no consistent message has been communicated, even among projects by the same organization. Most outreach initiatives target high school students with an eye toward "priming the engineering education pipeline." Less attention has been paid to elementary and middle school students, where efforts would serve a "mainline" function of promoting technological literacy and stimulating interest in mathematics and science. With the notable exception of National Engineers Week, most outreach programs have been local.

In general, messages targeting younger children attempt to convince them that mathematics and science are easy or fun and that engineering is challenging, exciting, hands-on, and rewarding. Messages for older, prospective college students tend to emphasize career potential. For the most part, these have been direct statements emphasizing the personal benefits of being an engineer.

A recurring theme in many messaging efforts is that engineering requires skills in mathematics and science. Frequently, these messages suggest that students must have an aptitude for and strong interest in these subjects to succeed in engineering.

CHANGING THE CONVERSATION

In collaboration with the committee, the consultants developed a positioning statement to guide future outreach activities by the engineering community (Box ES-1). This optimistic, inspirational statement emphasizes connections between engineering and ideas and possibilities, rather than engineering as a math and science based method of solving problems. The statement describes engineering as inherently creative and concerned with human welfare, as well as an emotionally satisfying calling. In short, the statement changes the tone and content of the conversation about engineering. A positioning statement is the conceptual foundation for a communications campaign, but it is not usually shared with the public.

BOX ES-1
New Positioning Statement

No profession unleashes the spirit of innovation like engineering. From research to real-world applications, engineers constantly discover how to improve our lives by creating bold new solutions that connect science to life in unexpected, forward-thinking ways. Few professions turn so many ideas into so many realities. Few have such a direct and positive effect on people's everyday lives. We are counting on engineers and their imaginations to help us meet the needs of the 21st century.

Findings from the Qualitative Research

Students in the focus groups and triads were asked to describe their images of engineers, their understanding of engineering, their reactions to examples of engineering, their views on current school subjects, and their hopes for future careers. Participants in the parent group were asked to describe their thoughts and ideas about career choices for their children. Both students and parents were also asked their reactions to several preliminary messaging "themes" (Box ES-2) based on the positioning statement.

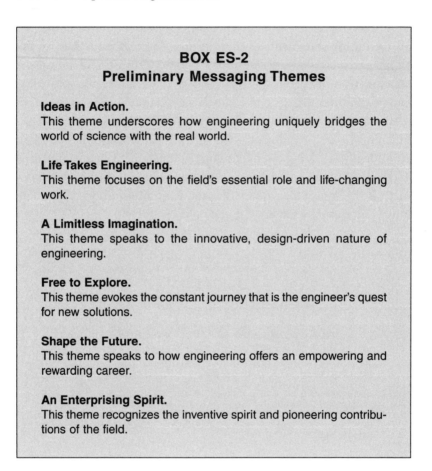

BOX ES-2
Preliminary Messaging Themes

Ideas in Action.
This theme underscores how engineering uniquely bridges the world of science with the real world.

Life Takes Engineering.
This theme focuses on the field's essential role and life-changing work.

A Limitless Imagination.
This theme speaks to the innovative, design-driven nature of engineering.

Free to Explore.
This theme evokes the constant journey that is the engineer's quest for new solutions.

Shape the Future.
This theme speaks to how engineering offers an empowering and rewarding career.

An Enterprising Spirit.
This theme recognizes the inventive spirit and pioneering contributions of the field.

Summary Findings: Students

- Most students understand that engineers "design and build things" but have a limited sense of what engineers actually do.
- Students have a generally positive impression of engineers, but many feel that they are not smart enough to become engineers.

- Many students believe engineering work is sedentary, performed mostly on computers, and involves little contact with other people.
- Most girls believe women can be engineers as well as men.
- When asked to name engineers, most students could only name men.
- Examples of engineering related to familiar objects and activities stimulated the most interest in learning more about engineering.
- "Making good money" was named most often as a career goal.[1] However, the idea of "making a difference" also had very strong appeal.

Summary Findings: Parents

- Most parents thought engineering would provide job security (e.g., good salary and benefits) and a career path for advancement and success.
- Parents tended to favor the practical messaging themes, reflecting their emphasis on job security for their children.

Findings from the Quantitative Research

To test the results of qualitative research, the committee collected quantitative data from an online survey administered to nearly 3,600 individuals. The survey instrument comprised six questions about views of engineering and engineers and four questions about the proposed messages and taglines that had been refined to reflect the results of the focus groups and triads (Box ES-3). The survey was administered in two phases: to an initial sample of teens and adults in December 2006 and an oversample of African American and Hispanic teens and adults in spring 2007.

All five messages were scored at least "somewhat appealing" by the overwhelming majority of adults and teens. The message with the

---

[1]By contrast, teens in the online survey rated the importance of salary second or third behind "interesting work" and "work that makes a difference, is meaningful."

BOX ES-3
Messages Tested in the Online Survey

Engineers make a world of difference.*
From new farming equipment and safer drinking water to electric cars and faster microchips, engineers use their knowledge to improve people's lives in meaningful ways.

Engineers are creative problem-solvers.
They have a vision for how something should work and are dedicated to making it better, faster, or more efficient.

Engineers help shape the future.
They use the latest science, tools, and technology to bring ideas to life.

Engineering is essential to our health, happiness, and safety.
From the grandest skyscrapers to microscopic medical devices, it is impossible to imagine life without engineering.

Engineers connect science to the real world.
They collaborate with scientists and other specialists (such as animators, architects, or chemists) to turn bold new ideas into reality.

---

*This message was inspired by a similar theme used to promote National Engineers Week.

highest "very appealing" rating among all groups was "Engineers make a world of difference." This message was also considered the "most believable" and "most relevant." In general, however, girls were less enthusiastic than boys about all of the messages.

"Engineers connect science to the real world" was given the fewest votes for "very appealing" among all groups and was the least "personally relevant" for all groups but African American adults. This finding was confirmed when survey participants were asked to choose a single "most appealing" message.

The survey also revealed some significant gender differences. For example, boys in the initial sample found "Engineering makes a world of difference" and "Engineers are creative problem solvers" equally appealing. Girls also found "Engineering makes a world of difference" the most appealing. However, the second most appealing message for girls was "Engineering is essential to our health, happiness, and safety." Girls ages 16 to 17 in the African American sample and all girls in the Hispanic sample found this second message significantly more appealing than did the boys in those groups.

Testing of Preliminary Taglines

In addition to messages, the online survey tested several preliminary taglines (Box ES-4). Because of time and funding constraints, the taglines had been developed intuitively from the results of the qualitative research, without the benefit of creative prototypes (such as posters, TV ads, or web pages). In addition, the taglines were only tested in the online surveys. Thus the results may not represent the best measure of their true potential. Nevertheless, several taglines tested well.

The tagline "Turning ideas into reality" tested well among all survey respondents. This straightforward tagline, which is consistent with the messages used to promote National Engineers Week, is more descriptive than evocative and conveys a direct message that does not require additional creative context. As a stand-alone *tagline*, it makes

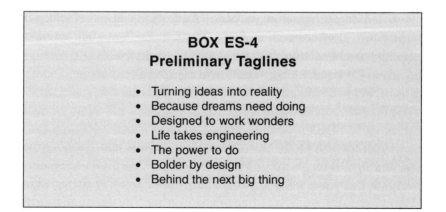

BOX ES-4
Preliminary Taglines

- Turning ideas into reality
- Because dreams need doing
- Designed to work wonders
- Life takes engineering
- The power to do
- Bolder by design
- Behind the next big thing

the most sense of the seven. It is interesting to note, however, that the phrase "ideas into reality" also appears in the full description of "Engineers connect science to the real world," which was the least appealing of the five tested messages, especially among women. This discrepancy reinforces the need for additional testing of taglines. A tagline that tested especially well among teens in the initial survey was "Because dreams need doing."

CONCLUSIONS AND RECOMMENDATIONS

Happily, our research showed that engineers do not have major image problems. In fact, contrary to the image engineers have of themselves, the public views engineering and engineers in a relatively positive light. Our research showed that fewer than 15 percent associated the words "boring" or "nerdy" with engineering. In fact, most adults and teens respect engineers and consider their work rewarding and important, but perhaps not enough to inspire them to become engineers.

We did find that the public has a poor idea of what engineers actually do on a day-to-day basis; and there is a strong sense that engineering is not "for everyone," and perhaps especially not for girls. Most current messages are framed to emphasize the strong links between engineering and just one of its attributes—the need for mathematics and science skills. In other words, current messages often ignore other vital characteristics of engineering, such as creativity, teamwork, and communication.

Based on our research, we can make a strong case that effective messaging will require audience segmentation. The "branding" of engineering must be modified to appeal to (1) teens in general, (2) teenage boys, and (3) teenage girls, as well as to (4) adults.

RECOMMENDATIONS

The committee's first two recommendations address how the positioning statement and messages should be used. These recommendations are immediately actionable by organizations interested in improving public understanding of engineering. The third and fourth recommendations, which suggest the need to refine the preliminary taglines and to develop a public relations "tool kit" for the engineering community, can be addressed in the near term and will require dedicated personnel and funding. Efforts to carry out the last recommendation, which proposes an ambitious, large-scale communications "campaign," can begin immediately, but successful implementation will require long-term, sustained effort by many organizations.

Using the Positioning Statement

Recommendation 1. To present an effective case for the importance of engineering and the value of an engineering education, the engineering community should engage in coordinated, consistent, effective communication to "reposition" engineering. Specifically, the engineering community should adopt and actively promote the positioning statement (Box 4-1) in this report, which emphasizes that engineering and engineers can make a difference in the world, rather than describing engineering in terms of required skills and personal benefits. The statement should not appear verbatim in external communications but should be used as a point of reference, or anchor, for all public outreach.

One of the most significant findings of this project is the strong association in the mind of the public between competency in mathematics and science and the ability to become an engineer. "Must be good at math and science" was by far the most frequently selected attribute of engineering in the online survey, suggesting that messages emphasizing this attribute have been understood by all adults and teenagers. Unfortunately, many of them appear to consider this a negative, a barrier to engineering studies. In keeping with this finding, our testing also showed that the weakest of the five tested messages portrayed engineers as "connecting science to the real world."

We conclude, therefore, that continuing to emphasize math and science in marketing or rebranding engineering is unnecessary and may damage rather than increase the appeal of engineering. The same can be said of messages that focus on the practical benefits of being an engineer, rather than the inspirational, optimistic aspects of engineering.

An example of how the medical profession is promoted may help illustrate the potential value of Recommendation 1. The medical profession does not market itself to young people by pointing out that they will have to study organic chemistry or by emphasizing the long, hard road to becoming a physician. The image of the physician is of a person who cures diseases and relieves human suffering.

When promoting engineering, our appeal should tap into the hopes and dreams of prospective students and the public. This approach would also have the virtue of placing math and science, correctly, as just two of a number of skills and dispositions, such as collaboration, communication, and teamwork, necessary to a successful engineer.

Adopting Tested Messages

Recommendation 2. The four messages that tested well in this project—"Engineers make a world of difference," "Engineers are creative problem solvers," "Engineers help shape the future," and "Engineering is essential to our health, happiness, and safety"—should be adopted by the engineering community in ongoing and new public outreach initiatives. The choice of a specific message should be based on the demographics of the target audience(s) and informed by the qualitative and quantitative data collected during this project.

Our research should not preclude others from pursuing message development, but we strongly feel that the rigorous process we used to generate our messages justifies their widespread use. In February 2008, the NAE launched a new website, Engineer Your Life (*www.engineeryourlife.org*), which aims to interest academically prepared high school girls in careers in engineering. The site used our message "Engineers make a world of difference" on its homepage and adopted other key words vetted in our research, such as creativity and problem-solving.

Using the Preliminary Taglines

Recommendation 3. More rigorous research should go forward to identify and test a small number of taglines for a nationwide engineering-awareness campaign. The taglines should be consistent with the positioning statement and messages developed through this project and should take into account differences among target populations. In the interest of encouraging coordination among outreach activities, the results of this research should be made widely available to the engineering community.

Given additional resources, it would have been useful in this project to develop and test more taglines in context and to test the contextualized taglines in focus groups. The results reported here should be viewed as preliminary, but the positive responses to several of our preliminary taglines in online testing suggest that they may be able to be used effectively for engineering-outreach projects.

Developing a Shared Public-Relations Resource

Recommendation 4. To facilitate the deployment of effective messages, an online public relations "tool kit" should be developed for the engineering community that includes information about research-based message-development initiatives and examples of how messages have and can be used effectively (e.g., in advertising, press releases, informational brochures, and materials for establishing institutional identity). The online site should also provide a forum for the sharing of information among organizations.

One reason ad hoc efforts to promote public awareness of engineering have had limited success, at best, is that they do not convey consistent messages. In addition, because of the discontinuity and lack of coordination among these activities, effective metrics cannot be used to refine messages or improve outreach. The committee believes that, in the short term, consistent use of messages, even by a modest number of organizations, would be a huge step forward in promoting a more positive public perception of engineering.

Launching a Campaign

Recommendation 5. A representative cross section of the engineering community should convene to consider funding, logistics, and other aspects of a coordinated, multiyear communications campaign to improve the public understanding of engineering.

Over the long term, the committee believes a more explicit, coordinated approach to public outreach is likely to yield better results than we have obtained so far. Thoughtful targeting of the messages and further refinement of taglines will be necessary, but not sufficient, for success. Messages and taglines must be embedded in a larger strategic framework—a communications campaign. The most effective campaigns are driven by a strong brand position communicated in a variety of ways, delivered by a variety of messengers, and supported by dedicated resources. Effective campaigns also measure the impact of their activities and, most important, are given enough time to succeed.

A campaign of the necessary size and duration to measurably improve the public understanding of engineering will require significant resources. Our consultants proposed a "conservative" price tag of $12 million to $25 million per year for two or three years. The committee believes that, although this may be enough to initiate a campaign, the long-term costs would be much higher.

Three concerns must be addressed for such an undertaking. First, resources on this scale are not likely to be provided by government or foundations. The engineering community, particularly large, influential, technology-focused corporations, must be enlisted to support the campaign.

Second, the committee believes that centralized planning will be necessary to ensure effective coordination and communication, which would require agreement by the major participants. National Engineers Week, a cooperative outreach venture in engineering, might be leveraged for this purpose. However, the creation of a new structure may be necessary to coordinate a campaign.

Third, metrics will be essential to determining the effectiveness of messages, strategies, and taglines. Although measuring the outcomes of public outreach efforts is notoriously difficult, a campaign of this scope must include a substantial evaluation component to determine what works and to improve upon elements that are not as effective as expected.

A FINAL WORD

The project described in this summary and expanded upon in the full report has followed a carefully designed process for developing messages for public understanding of engineering. The approach utilized the services of professionals in the fields of communications and market research, and it employed quantitative as well as qualitative research methods. To ensure balance and accuracy, the committee's report and its findings and recommendations were carefully reviewed by an outside group of experts. The rigor of the study process should reassure the engineering community—and others interested in this important topic—that there is now a tested set of tools available to promote a more positive image of the field.

The most significant outcome of this project is the recasting of engineering in the positioning statement. If it is adopted by the engineering community, it will not only reshape engineers' self-image, but will also empower engineers to communicate more confidently with the public.

As work continues on enriching, expanding, and disseminating messaging resources, the engineering community can take immediate action. Even if a national campaign is not immediately forthcoming, the creative implementation of the messages and taglines in this report can have an impact. Combined, consistent efforts by multiple organizations following the same "playbook" can create positive momentum toward making engineering more appealing and better understood by students, educators, parents, policy makers, and society at large. In this way, we may truly begin to change the conversation.

REFERENCES

Cunningham, C., and M. Knight. 2004. Draw an Engineer Test: Development of a Tool to Investigate Studentsí Ideas about Engineers and Engineering. Proceedings of the 2004 American Society for Engineering Education Annual Conference and Exposition. Salt Lake City, Utah, June 20–23. Washington, D.C.: ASEE.

Cunningham, C., C. Lachapelle, and A. Lindgren-Streicher. 2005. Assessing Elementary School Students Conceptions of Engineering and Technology. Proceedings of the 2005 American Society for Engineering Education Annual Conference and Exposition. Portland, Ore., June 12–15. Washington, D.C.: ASEE.

Harris Interactive. 2004. American Perspectives on Engineers and Engineering. Poll conducted for the American Association of Engineering Societies. Final report, February 13, 2004. Available online at *http://www.aaes.org/harris_2004_files/frame.htm.* (July 6, 2007)

Harris Interactive. 2006. Firefighters, doctors, and nurses top list as "most prestigious occupations," according to latest Harris Poll. The Harris Poll® #58, July 26, 2006. Available online at *http://harrisinteractive.com/harris_poll/index.asp?PID=685.* (July 6, 2007)

NAE (National Academy of Engineering). 2002. Raising Public Awareness of Engineering. L. Davis and R. Gibbin, eds. Washington, D.C.: The National Academies Press.

NAE and NRC (National Research Council). 2002. Technically Speaking: Why All Americans Need to Know More About Technology. Washington, D.C.: National Academy Press.

INTRODUCTION

1

Considerable efforts have been undertaken in the United States to improve the public understanding of engineering (PUE). A survey by the National Academy of Engineering (NAE) in 2002 of 177 organizations involved in public understanding of engineering activities revealed that they spend an estimated $400 million annually (NAE, 2002). However, the actual national investment can be assumed to be much higher, because the survey is believed to have reached only a fraction of the institutions that have PUE initiatives.

Despite these efforts, the impact of engineering on our daily lives, the nature of what engineers do, and the opportunities available through an engineering education are still largely unknown to most Americans. Educational researchers have found that K–12 teachers and students generally have a poor understanding of what engineers do (Cunningham and Knight, 2004; Cunningham et al., 2005, 2006). Polling data comparing scientists and engineers show that the public sees engineers as being more responsible for creating economic growth and preserving national security than scientists, as well as more likely to make strong leaders. However, engineers are not perceived to be as engaged with societal and community concerns or to play as great a role in saving lives (Table 1-1). And when the relative prestige of all professions is tallied, engineering falls in the middle of the pack, well below medicine, nursing, science, and teaching (Table 1-2).

Although engineers, engineering educators, and the organizations that represent them want people to have more accurate and positive impressions of them, there are other, more important reasons for improving the public understanding of engineering. Some knowledge about how engineering work is done, for example, is fundamental to technological literacy. To be fully capable and confident in a technology-dependent society, every citizen should understand something of the process of engineering and how engineering and science, among

TABLE 1-1 Comparative Characteristics Associated with Engineers and Scientists, 2003 and 1998

	Engineers	Scientists	Neither	Don't Know	Decline to Answer
Creates economic growth					
2003	69%	25%	2%	3%	*
1998	51%	25%	—	5%	1%
Preserves national security					
2003	59%	29%	5%	6%	1%
1998	36%	22%	—	9%	2%
Would make a strong leader					
2003	56%	32%	6%	5%	*
1998	47%	28%	—	8%	3%
Saves lives					
2003	14%	82%	1%	2%	*
1998	6%	65%	—	3%	21%
Is sensitive to societal concerns					
2003	28%	61%	5%	5%	*
1998	47%	57%	—	8%	3%
Cares about the community					
2003	37%	51%	5%	6%	1%
1998	24%	46%	—	9%	12%

NOTE: Numbers from 1998 do not add up to 100 because respondents chose from three answers: engineers, scientists, and technicians. Some numbers from 2003 do not add to 100 due to rounding.
*Less than 1 percent.
SOURCE: Adapted from Harris Interactive, 2004.

TABLE 1-2 Percent of Americans Who Rate Selected Professions as
Having "Very Great Prestige," 2006

Profession	Percent	Profession	Percent
Firefighter	63%	Architect	27%
Doctor	58%	Athlete	23%
Nurse	55%	Lawyer	21%
Scientist	54%	Entertainer	18%
Teacher	52%	Accountant	17%
Military officer	51%	Banker	17%
Police officer	43%	Journalist	16%
Priest	40%	Union leader	12%
Farmer	36%	Actor	10%
Engineer	34%	Stock broker	11%
Member of Congress	28%	Real estate agent	6%

SOURCE: Adapted from Harris Interactive, 2006.

other factors, lead to the development of technologies (NAE and NRC, 2002; AAAS, 1990).

A number of important public policy issues, from global warming to the marketing of genetically modified foods, involve scientific and technical issues. Decision making on these and other topics will involve trade-offs, as we attempt to simultaneously manage limited resources while sustaining quality of life. Public discourse and the democratic process could be enhanced if citizens understood more about how engineers are trained and what the practice of engineering entails. Technological literacy also is important to consumer decision making. Americans are often the first adopters of new technologies, and part of that acceptance depends on understanding the engineering process. Thus improved public understanding of engineering could enhance consumer decision making.

Improved public understanding of engineering may also support U.S. efforts to maintain our capacity for technological innovation, an issue that has received considerable attention recently (Council on Competitiveness, 2004; NAS et al., 2007; PCAST, 2004). Although there are many aspects of this challenge, two important conditions for sustaining U.S. innovative capacity are improving undergraduate engineering education (NAE, 2005a) and increasing investment in basic engineering research (NAE, 2005b). Effective action in both areas will depend partly on how well policy makers and the public understand what engineering is and how it contributes to economic development, quality of life, national security, and health—information that could be conveyed through effective messaging.

A related concern is the rapid increase in scientists and engineers in other nations, particularly China and India. For example, the number of graduates with four-year degrees in engineering, computer science (CS), and information technology (IT) in China more than doubled from 2000 to 2004 (Wadhwa et al., 2007). However, because of differences in methods of data collection and in defining engineering, it is difficult to compare the absolute numbers of four-year engineering degrees awarded in China and India to those awarded in the United States. In the 2003–2004 academic year, for bachelor's degrees in engineering, CS, and IT combined, Wadhwa et al. (2007) estimate that the United States graduated 137, 437, India 139,000, and China 361,270.

The overall number of engineering degrees granted in the United States, which had been dropping, has gone up in recent years, although not to its historic high in 1985 (Figure 1-1). According to one estimate,

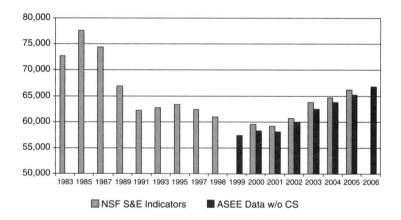

FIGURE 1-1 Engineering bachelor's degrees awarded in the United States, 1983–2006.
NOTE: Bachelor's degrees in computer science (CS) have been subtracted from the original ASEE data (Gibbons) to ensure comparability with NSF data.
SOURCES: Gibbons, 2006; NSF, 2006a.

the U.S. engineering workforce is expected to increase by 13 percent from 2004 to 2014 (CPST, 2006). However, the accuracy of this projection will be affected by several factors, such as participation levels of foreign-born individuals in the U.S. engineering enterprise, the off-shoring of U.S. engineering jobs (NAE, 2008), and engineer retirements in such sectors as defense and aerospace. Thus it is very difficult to predict the long-term demand or supply of engineers in the United States.

Although researchers and policy makers disagree on the nature and extent of the engineering "shortage" in the United States, few dispute the need to attract capable students, especially girls and certain minorities, into technical careers. Women, African Americans, Hispanics, Native Americans, and some Asian American groups are significantly underrepresented in engineering, based on their proportions in the population at large (Box 1-1). If current demographic trends continue, by 2050 almost half the U.S. population will be non-white (U.S. Census Bureau, 2002). In the future, engineering solutions will have to be acceptable to this increasingly diverse population, and the engineering profession will have to draw more heavily on underrepresented groups for the country to maintain, let alone increase, its technological capability (NAE, 2004). Thus messages that effectively encourage girls and underrepresented minorities to consider careers in engineering could be crucial to U.S. success and leadership in the future.

MESSAGES TO PROMOTE THE PUBLIC UNDERSTANDING OF ENGINEERING

In the NAE report *Raising Public Awareness of Engineering* (2002), "message," in the context of public relations, was defined as "a statement that helps convey a positive image, usually either of a company or a specific product." In well-designed communications strategies, messages are repeated over time, because public perceptions are influenced most by repeated exposure to consistently expressed ideas. Although neither engineering nor the public understanding of engineering is a corporate entity or—strictly speaking—a product, messaging is nevertheless germane in this context. Indeed, effective messaging is a

BOX 1-1
Selected Data for Women, African Americans, Hispanics, and Native Americans in Engineering

Women

Proportion of U.S. population, 2005 (est.):	**50.7 percent**
Proportion enrolled in degree-granting institutions, 2004:	**57.4 percent**
Proportion of bachelor's degrees in engineering, 2004:	**20.5 percent**
Proportion of tenured/tenure-track appointments on U.S. engineering faculties, 2005:	**10.6 percent**
Proportion employed as engineers, 2003:	**11.0 percent**

African Americans

Proportion of U.S. population, 2004:	**12.8 percent**
Proportion enrolled in degree-granting institutions, 2004:	**12.5 percent**
Proportion of bachelor's degrees in engineering earned, 2004	**5.3 percent**
Proportion of tenured/tenure-track appointments on U.S. engineering faculties, 2005:	**2.3 percent**
Proportion employed as engineers, 2003:	**3.1 percent**

Hispanics

Proportion of U.S. population, 2004:	**14.1 percent**
Proportion enrolled in degree-granting institutions, 2004:	**10.5 percent**
Proportion of bachelor's degrees in engineering, 2004:	**7.4 percent**
Proportion of tenured/tenure-track professors on U.S. engineering faculties, 2005:	**3.2 percent**
Proportion employed as engineers, 2003:	**4.9 percent**

Native Americans

Proportion of U.S. population, 2004:	**1.0 percent**
Proportion enrolled in degree-granting institutions, 2004:	**1.0 percent**
Proportion of bachelor's degrees in engineering, 2004:	**0.6 percent**
Proportion of tenured/tenure-track professors on U.S. engineering faculties, 2005:	**0.2 percent**
Proportion employed as engineers, 2003:	**0.3 percent**

SOURCES: NSF, 2005a, b, 2006a, b; U.S. Census Bureau, 2002, 2005; DOEd, 2006a, b.

necessary—although not a sufficient—method of promoting public understanding of engineering efforts.

The 2002 NAE report catalogs a large number of messages on a variety of themes that organizations involved in public understanding of engineering have used to promote their activities. The four major themes are: the value and nature of engineering and engineers; the academic skills necessary to pursue engineering as a career; employment opportunities in engineering; and the connection between engineering and quality of life.

The number and variety of messages leads to several conclusions. First, no apparent effort has been made in the engineering community to develop consistent messages. Second, few organizations involved in promoting public understanding of engineering have developed their messages in a systematic, scientific way or tested the effectiveness of their messages. Third, no convincing evidence shows that messaging efforts to date have significantly improved public understanding of engineering.

We know that a public image is not "everything," as the advertisement for Nikon cameras asserted more than a decade ago, but neither is it inconsequential. In the case of engineering, data collected for this project show that the public view of engineering is not strongly negative. At the same time, the data suggest that public perceptions of engineering are based on a limited idea of what it takes to *do* engineering (e.g., skill in mathematics and science) rather than what it means to *be* an engineer (e.g., to work creatively in teams to develop technologies that improve people's lives).

PRIMER ON MARKET RESEARCH: LEXICON AND METHODS

A professional marketing firm was hired to ensure that the committee took a professional approach to improving public understanding of engineering. In addition, committee members were obliged to learn marketing terminology. Learning the vocabulary for any subject requires not only memorizing terms, but also acquiring an understanding of the underlying concepts and methodology. In this section, we outline the essential terms and marketing concepts the committee used in preparing this report and recommendations.

Definition of a Brand

In this project, we were looking for the best way to brand engineering. Although the word *brand* seems familiar, it is used in a specific way in this report. By brand we mean an association of specific traits in a person's mind that induces behavior. A simple way of understanding this concept might be as a warranty—a promise to perform or deliver. For example, the McDonald's brand promises clean restaurants and food of a known quality. We use this brand as a shortcut in decision making. For example, when traveling on the road, we rely on McDonald's promise to provide a quick, adequate meal. The same thing happens with brands in a grocery or hardware store. As we shop, we make quick judgments based on a brand's promise or warranty.

Contemporary marketing practice and theory support branding that goes beyond traditional ideas of a product. For example, entire industries have attempted to remake their public image using branding techniques. The dairy industry's "Got Milk" campaign (*www.bodybymilk.com*) uses well-known sports and entertainment figures to cultivate a wholesome brand image for milk drinkers. Similarly, the cotton industry's "Fabric of Our Lives" campaign (*www.thefabricofourlives.com*) ties a broad range of cotton-based products to aspects of daily life. Marketing has been used by public health officials to brand desirable behaviors, such as healthy eating in adults (i.e., the Food and Drug Administration's "Calories Count" campaign; FDA, 2004) and exercise in children (i.e., the Centers for Disease Control and Prevention's "Verb, It's What You Do" campaign; *www.verbnow.com*).

Some professions have a clear brand identity. Physicians, for examples, are "healers." Teachers are "educators." For professions that do not have a clear brand identity, the public may provide one. Lobbyists and others operating in the political sector can be known as "influence peddlers." And for those in public relations, derisive terms like "flack" and "spin doctor" are common. In the case of engineering, although negative terms like "nerd" and "boring" are part of the brand image, our research and research by others indicate the larger problem is a lack of understanding of what engineers do rather than a negative impression of the field. The actuarial field has a similar concern and has undertaken branding efforts to better communicate to the public how actuaries add value (Beuerlein, 2006). Nurses in the United Kingdom, concerned about their relatively low status and poor image, recently launched a "Nursing the Future" campaign (*www.nursingthefuture. org.uk/index.php*). To attract students and counter the stuffy image of accountants, the American Institute of Certified Public Accountants developed the "Start Here Go Places" campaign (*www.startheregoplaces. com*).

In this study, we considered the following brand attributes: brand message, the promise the brand communicates; brand image, how the brand is marketed; and brand experience, how the message is brought to life and made concrete.

The Positioning Statement

A *positioning statement* is essential for creating a brand. It lays out how one wants the brand to be perceived and provides the core message to be delivered in every medium. A typical positioning statement answers seven core questions about a brand:

1. Who are you?
2. What business are you in?
3. What people do you serve?
4. What are the special needs of the people you serve?
5. Who are your competitors?
6. What makes you different from your competitors?
7. What unique benefit does a user derive from your service or product?

To illustrate how a position statement works, consider a high-end store like Bloomingdale's. The position statement (Beckwith, 1997) reads:

> Bloomingdale's (*who*) is a fashion-focused department store (*what business*) for trend-conscious, upper-middle-class shoppers (*who served*) looking for high-end products (*special needs*). Unlike other department stores (*competitors*), Bloomingdale's provides unique merchandise in a theatrical setting (*the difference*), which makes shopping entertaining (*unique benefit*).

Note that this statement never appears explicitly in Bloomingdale's ads or marketing. The purpose of a positioning statement is to guide decisions about how to deliver a brand message. A marketing firm uses the statement to create the elements of a campaign. For example, Bloomingdale's highlights items in its ads and creates displays in its stores that reinforce the idea of "shopping entertainment."

A positioning statement, of course, applies not only to traditional stores like Bloomingdale's, but can also be a powerful tool, for example, in a high-tech industry. In 1991, Intel Corporation launched a brand campaign for its computer processors. At the time, few consumers had any idea what a microprocessor was, let alone a strong brand identification or preference for a particular type of processor. Most consumers cared as much about who made their processors as they did about who built the engines in their cars.

This presented a dilemma for Intel, which wanted to reap the benefits of its advances in chip design. So, the firm decided to brand its processors, thus linking Intel and its innovations. This was a revolutionary idea, because at the time, consumers knew next to nothing about microprocessors. A measure of the campaign's success is that today people discuss the speed of their processors, and even mention their name.

We can imagine Intel using something like the following positioning statement, which we crafted based on the history of the Intel Inside® Program (Intel Corporation, 2008), to create its brand:

> Intel (*who*) produces microprocessors (*what business*) for end users of personal computers (*who served*) looking for the best technology (*special need*) linking words like "leading technology" and "reliability" (*unique benefit*) with Intel microprocessors rather than other producers of microprocessors (*competitors*).

Messages and Taglines

The key elements of messaging campaigns, like Bloomingdale's and Intel's, are *messages* and *taglines*, which are easily confused. The message, the longer and more detailed of the two, is often a complete sentence that clearly articulates a brand promise. For example, the message of Anadin™, a pain killer, makes an explicit promise in, "Nothing acts faster than Anadin™." In contrast, a tagline is a short phrase, rarely a complete sentence, that creates an image in the consumer's mind. One committee member described taglines as "concretely vague," somewhat like a Madison Avenue haiku that resonates emotionally with consumers.

Intel's now-ubiquitous tagline is "Intel Inside," which cleverly draws attention to a tiny, rarely seen, but essential component of the computer "brain." Ford Motor Company's tagline for its Lincoln Town Car is "Signature of Success," which taps into the self-image of consumers who might purchase these luxury cars.

Two examples from this project can help clarify the differences between messages and taglines. As noted above, we engaged a marketing firm to develop and test engineering messages and taglines. One message we tested was:

> Engineers make a world of difference. From new farming equipment and safer drinking water to electric cars and faster microchips, engineers use their knowledge to improve people's lives in meaningful ways.

One of several taglines we tested reads:

> Because dreams need doing

To develop and test messages and taglines, the marketing company conducted research in the form of focus groups and surveys.

The Role of Research

Marketing research suggests reasonable actions to take in creating a brand, rather than charting a definitive course to success. Much like social science research, marketing research reveals trends that can simplify a complex whole by breaking it into manageable parts. Research does not tell us which branding elements to use, but it provides insights that inform, rather than replace, decision making. Marketing research serves two main purposes in creating a branding campaign.

First, marketing research reveals how prospective consumers perceive a product or service. One might naively assume that a firm can state a position and then broadcast that position in all of its marketing. In reality, a marketer does not create a position de novo, but links a new position to an old position that already exists in the consumer's mind.

For example, in the 1960s, Avis wanted to let potential customers know that it offered better service than Hertz, the top rental-car company, but research revealed that consumers did not find this claim credible. In fact, consumers always thought of Avis as second to Hertz. In an ingenious advertising campaign, Avis used the tagline, "We're number two, so we try harder." Because this tagline connected to an idea already in consumers' minds, it instantly resonated with them, and Avis' revenues skyrocketed (*Wall Street Journal,* 1969). This is a clear example of how a marketing firm used research to get a good picture of the messaging landscape and created a tagline that linked a new position to an old one.

The second way marketing firms use research is to test messages and taglines. Testing can reveal the most popular or appealing brand elements, but more important, it can reveal unanticipated problems. For example, a tagline that appeals to a marketer and client may have unintended negative connotations for the target audience.

In our research, we were particularly interested in developing an exhaustive, fine-grained description of the perceptions of different groups about engineering as a profession. This required the systematic collection of data from well-defined sample groups using standardized questionnaires that would provide a basis for making comparisons.

The paramount criteria for evaluating all social science research are *validity* and *reliability. Validity* means that our results tap into the underlying behaviors or attitudes we want to measure. Can a survey questionnaire, for example, adequately assess people's complex attitudes toward engineering? *Reliability,* on the other hand, refers to consistency of measurement. Can we administer the same questionnaire consistently to a large number of respondents, for instance, without contaminating our results because of differences in how the interviews were conducted?

All researchers must make trade-offs between reliability and validity. Standardized surveys are very reliable in how they are administered and in how they measure underlying constructs, such as attitudes and behaviors. At the same time, their validity is limited, because they reduce complex attitudes to short questions with answers that are often forced into predefined numerical scales.

The problem is often reversed for focus groups and other qualitative methods, which enable us to explore behaviors and attitudes in great depth and include a good deal of contextual information. Therefore, they produce more valid results than standardized surveys. However, the very fact that they take into account individual differences and complexities diminishes their reliability for comparisons among different groups. The fact that we used a semi-structured interview protocol for the focus groups corrected somewhat for this limitation.

For our project, therefore, we "triangulated" these methods, combining qualitative approaches, such as focus groups, with quantitative data collection using systematic population surveys. This enabled us to leverage the specific advantages of each method in terms of reliability and validity and, at the same time, minimize their weaknesses by comparing results. (The committee discusses other technical issues, including factors that affect generalizability of data, in an annex to this chapter.)

THE NAE MESSAGING PROJECT

This project is based on the hypothesis that concise, effective messaging can help correct misconceptions about, and improve the image of, engineers and engineering. Effective messages will be a compelling and consistent way for the engineering community to promote itself to diverse audiences. NAE recognizes that effective messages are a critical (but not sufficient) element in cultivating greater public awareness. Messaging must be a component in a sustained engineering-community-wide campaign that also includes improving undergraduate engineering education and increasing investment in basic engineering research.

Goal and Objectives of the Project

The stated goal of this project, funded by the National Science Foundation (NSF) and small, supplemental grants from the Georgia Institute of Technology and the S.D. Bechtel, Jr. Foundation, is to encourage coordinated, consistent, effective communication by the engineering community about the role, importance, and career potential of engineering to a variety of audiences, including school children, parents, teachers, and counselors. The project hopes to achieve three specific objectives:

- Identify a small number of messages that appear likely to lead to a better understanding of engineering.
- Test the effectiveness of these messages in a variety of audiences.
- Disseminate testing results to the engineering community.

This project did not have the goal of developing metrics for measuring the effectiveness of messaging efforts. Nevertheless, it is reasonable to ask what one might look for as evidence of "improvement" in public understanding of engineering. One indicator of improvement would be the number and diversity of organizations using this report to shape their engineering outreach. Over time, we would hope to see growth in this set of organizations, and that might be measured through surveys of the engineering community. The committee believes that effective messaging will equip people with a positive and authentic vocabulary for describing and thinking about engineering. In addition, effective messaging should have an impact on student views about engineering as a career option. One approach for gathering this kind of information would be a longitudinal study, combined with "dipstick" surveys before, during, and after the deployment of new messages. Such a study could determine the extent to which the public recognizes the new messages or associates certain key words, such as creativity, with engineering, and it could probe students for how messages are influencing their views about career and college choice. Less direct evidence of impact might be obtained by tracking changes in responses to periodic national surveys, such as those on professional prestige conducted by Harris Interactive; commissioning new surveys, for example, of high school students views about engineering; or analyzing factors leading to changes in enrollments in engineering schools.

Public Outreach

During the course of this project, the committee solicited feedback in two ways. First, committee members and project staff made presentations about the project at meetings where the topic of public understanding of engineering was likely to resonate. These events included the April 2007 meeting of the NAE Council; the annual Convocation of Professional Engineering Societies and the NAE in May 2007, which brought together the presidents, presidents-elect, and executive directors of major national engineering professional associations to discuss issues of mutual interest; the May 2007 and April 2008 meetings of the advisory committee to the Engineering Directorate of the NSF, which funded the project; the June 2007 annual meeting of the American Society for Engineering Education; and the January 2008 meeting of the Association of Independent Technical Universities. At each event, the goals and research findings of the project generated considerable discussion.

To obtain feedback from a wider cross section of the engineering community and the general population, in March 2007 the committee posted a report by the project consultants, Bemporad Baranowski Marketing Group/Global Strategy Group, on the NAE website that provided background material and summarized the findings of the qualitative research and the survey's initial sample. (Results of the oversamples of African American and Hispanic teens and adults were not available until June, too late to allow for public comment.)

The committee notified a number of groups about the posting, including NAE members; the National Academies Teacher Advisory Council; a number of engineering societies (e.g., American Society of Mechanical Engineers, Institute for Electrical and Electronics Engineers, American Society of Civil Engineers, National Society of Professional Engineers, National Society of Black Engineers, Society of Women Engineers, American Society of Engineering Education); the International Technology Education Association, which represents K–12 technology education teachers; the Association of Science-Technology Centers, which represents many science and technology museums; and the National Association for College Admission Counseling.

From March through June 2007, the committee received comments on the consultants' report from more than 80 organizations and individuals. The great majority of these were from engineers, including 10 NAE members, three deans of schools of engineering, and individual engineers who teach in universities or work in industry. The committee also received comments from a handful of K–12 teachers, mostly teachers of technology, mathematics, and science.

The comments included a number of suggestions for using the messages, arguments in favor of particular messages, and proposals for conducting a large-scale campaign to improve public understanding of engineering. There were also a number of insightful comments on issues not directly considered in this project, such as the lack of opportunities for K–12 students to study engineering and the quality of post-secondary engineering education. Where appropriate, references to these comments are included in the committee's report.

The Report

Chapter 2 describes the committee's efforts to develop a positioning statement and preliminary message themes as guidelines for the research phase of the project. Chapter 3 presents the results of that research. Chapter 4 provides the committee's conclusions and recommendations. Appendix A contains short biographies of committee members, Appendix B is the moderator's guide for the in-depth interviews, Appendix C is the moderator's guide for the parent focus groups, Appendix D is the moderator's guide for the teen focus groups, Appendix E is the moderator's guide for the youth triads, and Appendix F is the online survey. A separate CD contains complete data tables for the online survey and a PDF version of the full report.

REFERENCES

AAAS (American Association for the Advancement of Science). 1990. Chapter 3, The nature of technology, and Chapter 8, The designed world in Science for All Americans. New York: Oxford University Press.
Beckwith, H. 1997. Selling the Invisible: A Field Guide to Modern Marketing. New York: Warner Books.

Beuerlein, R. 2006. One voice, one brand. Presidential address. The Actuary Magazine. April/May 2006. Available online at *http://www.soa.org/library/newsletters/ the-actuary-magazine/2006/april/act-pres-address.aspx.* (January 20, 2008)

Council on Competitiveness. 2004. Innovate America—Thriving in a World of Challenge and Change. Available online at *http://www.compete.org/pdf/NII_Interim_Report. pdf.* (July 28, 2005)

Couper, M.P. 2000. Review: Web surveys: A review of issues and approaches. Public Opinion Quarterly 64(4): 464–494.

CPST (Commission on Professionals in Science and Technology). 2006. STEM Employment Forecasts and Distributions Among Employment Sectors. STEM Workforce Data Project: Report No. 7. Available online at *http://www.cpst.org/STEM/STEM7_ Report.pdf.* (April 28, 2008)

Crocket, R.O., and S.E. Ante. 2007. Equal opportunity speedway: African Americans are snapping up broadband—and closing the digital divide. Business Week, May 21, 2007, p. 44.

Cunningham, C., and M. Knight. 2004. Draw an Engineer Test: Development of a Tool to Investigate Students' Ideas about Engineers and Engineering. Proceedings of the 2004 American Society for Engineering Education Annual Conference and Exposition. Salt Lake City, Utah, June 20–23. Washington, D.C.: ASEE.

Cunningham, C., C. Lachapelle, and A. Lindgren-Streicher. 2005. Assessing Elementary School Students Conceptions of Engineering and Technology. Proceedings of the 2005 American Society for Engineering Education Annual Conference and Exposition. Portland, Ore., June 12–15. Washington, D.C.: ASEE.

Cunningham, C., C. Lachapelle, and A. Lindgren-Streicher. 2006. Elementary Teachers' Understandings of Engineering and Technology. Proceedings of the 2006 American Society for Engineering Education Annual Conference and Exposition. Chicago, Ill., June 18–21. Washington, D.C.: ASEE.

DOEd (United States Department of Education). 2006a. National Center for Education Statistics. Digest of Education Statistics, 2005 (NCES 2006-030), Table 205. Available online at *http://nces.ed.gov/fastfacts/display.asp?id=98.* (October 26, 2007)

DOEd. 2006b. National Center for Education Statistics. Digest of Education Statistics, 2005 (NCES 2006-030), Table 170. Available online at *http://nces.ed.gov/programs/digest/ d05/tables/dt05_170.asp.* (October 26, 2007)

FDA (Food and Drug Administration). 2004. HHS unveils FDA strategy to help reduce obesity. New "calories count" approach builds on HHS' education, research efforts. Press release, March 12, 2004. Available online at: *http://www.fda.gov/bbs/topics/ news/2004/hhs_031204.html.* (January 20, 2008)

Gibbons, M.T. 2006. Engineering by the Numbers. Sample from the 2006 Profiles of Engineering and Engineering Technology Colleges, American Association of Engineering Education. Available online at *http://www.asee.org/publications/profiles/ upload/2006ProfileEng.pdf.* (January 4, 2008)

Harris Interactive. 2004. American Perspectives on Engineers and Engineering. Poll conducted for the American Association of Engineering Societies. Final report, February 13, 2004. Available online at *http://www.aaes.org/harris_2004_files/frame.htm.* (July 6, 2007)

Harris Interactive. 2006. Firefighters, doctors and nurses top list as "most prestigious occupations," according to latest Harris poll. *The Harris Poll®* #58, July 26, 2006. Available online at *http://www.harrisinteractive.com/harris_poll/index.asp?PID=685.* (July 6, 2007)

ICR (International Communications Research). 2007. Sampling Tolerances for Survey Percentages. Available online at *http://www.icrsurvey.com/SamplingChart.pdf.* (October 26, 2007)

Intel Corporation. 2008. Intel Inside® Program—Anatomy of a Brand Campaign. Available online at: *http://www.intel.com/pressroom/intel_inside.htm.* (January 4, 2008)

Lenhart, A., M. Madden, and P. Hitlin. 2005. Teens and Technology—Youth Are Leading the Transition to a Fully Wired and Mobile Nation. Pew Internet & American Life Project. Available online at *http://www.pewinternet.org/pdfs/PIP_Teens_Tech_July2005web.pdf.* (July 17, 2007)

Madden, M. 2006. Data Memo on Internet Penetration and Impact. Pew Internet & American Life Project. Available online at *http://www.pewinternet.org/pdfs/PIP_Internet_Impact.pdf.* (July 16, 2007)

NAE (National Academy of Engineering). 2002. Raising Public Awareness of Engineering. L. Davis and R. Gibbin, eds. Washington, D.C.: The National Academies Press.

NAE. 2005a. Educating the Engineer of 2020: Adapting Engineering to the New Century. Committee on the Engineer of 2020, Phase II, and the Committee on Engineering Education. Washington, D.C.: The National Academies Press.

NAE. 2005b. Engineering Research and America's Future: Meeting the Challenges of a Global Economy. Committee to Assess the Capacity of the U.S. Engineering Research Enterprise. Washington, D.C.: The National Academies Press.

NAE. 2004. The Engineering of 2020—Visions of Engineering in the New Century. Washington, D.C.: The National Academies Press.

NAE. 2008. The Offshoring of Engineering: Facts, Myths, Unknowns, and Potential Implications. Committee on the Offshoring of Engineering. Washington, D.C.: The National Academies Press.

NAE and NRC (National Research Council). 2002. Technically Speaking: Why All Americans Need to Know More About Technology. Washington, D.C.: National Academy Press.

NAS (National Academy of Sciences), NAE, IOM (Institute of Medicine). 2007. Rising Above the Gathering Storm: Energizing and Employing America for a Brighter Economic Future. Washington, D.C.: The National Academies Press.

NSF (National Science Foundation). 2005a. Science and Engineering Degrees: 1966–2004. Table 47: Engineering degrees awarded, by degree level and sex of recipient, 1966–2004. Available online at *http://www.nsf.gov/statistics/nsf07307/pdf/tab47.pdf.* (January 4, 2008)

NSF. 2005b. Women, minorities, and persons with disabilities in science and engineering. Table C-7: Racial/ethnic distribution of S&E bachelor's degrees awarded to U.S. Citizens and permanent residents, by field: 1995–2004. Available online at *http://www.nsf.gov/statistics/wmpd/pdf/tabc-7.pdf.* (January 4, 2008)

NSF. 2006a. Science and engineering indicators 2006. Appendix Table 2-26. Available online at *http://nsf.gov/statistics/seind06/append/c2/at02-26.xls.* (September 18, 2007)

NSF. 2006b. Science and engineering indicators 2006, Figure 3-26. Available online at *http://www.nsf.gov/statistics/seind06/c3/c3s1.htm#c3s1l11.* (January 4, 2008)

PCAST (President's Council of Advisors on Science and Technology). 2004. Sustaining the Nation's Innovation Ecosystem: Maintaining the Strength of Our Science and Engineering Capabilities. Available online at *http://ostp.gov/pcast/ FINALPCASTSECAPABILITIESPACKAGE.pdf.* (July 28, 2005)

Sheldon, H., C. Graham, N. Pothecary, and F. Rasul. 2007. Increasing response rates amongst black and minority ethnic and seldom heard groups: A review of the literature relevant to the National Acute Patients' Survey. Picker Institute Europe. Available online at *www.nhssurveys.org/docs/Inpatient_Survey_2007_Increasing_ response_rates8.pdf.* (June 30, 2007)

U.S. Census Bureau. 2002. Current Population Reports: Population Projections of the United States by Age, Sex, Race, and Hispanic Origin: 1995 to 2050. Table J, p. 13. Available online at *http://www.census.gov/prod/1/pop/p25-1130.pdf.* (September 18, 2007)

U.S. Census Bureau. 2005. Population Profile of the United States: Dynamic Version. Race and Hispanic Origin in 2005. Available online at *http://www.census.gov/population/ pop-profile/dynamic/RACEHO.pdf.* (October 26, 2007)

Wadhwa, V., G. Gereffi, B. Rissing, and R. Ong. 2007. Where the engineers are. Issues in Science and Technology (Spring): 73–84.

Wall Street Journal. 1969. Doyle Dane took over the Avis account six years ago. Since then Avis' business has quadrupled. May 12, 1969, p. 6.

ANNEX
GENERALIZABILITY OF SURVEY DATA

Generalizability, the capability of making inferences from a sample to the target population, is an essential aspect of survey research. The most commonly used inferential statistic is *sampling tolerance,* often called the *margin of error.* We prefer the former term, because the margin of error suggests, incorrectly, that there is something wrong with the data, whereas sampling tolerance refers to the difference between results from the sample and results anticipated in the target population as a whole.

Sampling tolerance varies by the size of the sample (the larger the sample, the smaller the tolerance) and the reported percentage response to a particular survey question (the closer the response percentage is to 50 percent, the larger the sampling tolerance). Table 1-3 illustrates how these factors affect tolerance for individual data points. Sampling tolerances are often expressed as plus or minus values (+/−), or ranges, around the data point of interest.

TABLE 1-3 Sampling Tolerances for Single Samples

| Sample Size | Reported Percents | | | | |
	10% or 90%	20% or 80%	30% or 70%	40% or 60%	50%
100	5.9	7.8	9.0	9.6	9.8
200	4.2	5.5	6.4	6.8	6.9
300	3.4	4.5	5.2	5.5	5.7
400	2.9	3.9	4.5	4.8	4.9
500	2.6	3.5	4.0	4.3	4.4
600	2.4	3.2	3.7	3.9	4.0
700	2.2	3.0	3.4	3.6	3.7
800	2.1	2.8	3.2	3.4	3.5
900	2.0	2.6	3.0	3.2	3.3
1000	1.9	2.5	2.8	3.0	3.1
1500	1.6	2.0	2.4	2.5	2.6
2000	1.3	1.8	2.1	2.2	2.2
5000	0.8	1.1	1.3	1.4	1.4

SOURCE: ICR, 2007.

Our surveys had a 95 percent *confidence level*, the industry standard. This means that we can be 95 percent certain that the value for the true population falls somewhere within the margin of error around what we observed in our sample. For example, as Table 1-3 shows, for a sample of 600 people, if 20 percent chose a particular answer choice, the sampling tolerance would be +/– 3.2 percent, and the answer range would be between 17.8 percent and 23.2 percent. This means that we can predict with 95 percent certainty that the percentage of individuals in the population we drew our sample from fall within the calculated range. The same principle applies when two data points are compared, although the calculation is more involved, particularly if the sample sizes vary. In this case, the difference between the numbers is considered *statistically significant* if it exceeds the sampling tolerance.

The correct calculation of inferential statistics depends on each respondent having the same, known chance of being selected into the sample. For example, to survey the opinions of the U.S. population as a whole, the survey sample would include representative numbers of people, in terms of age, gender, race or ethnicity, and geographic location, just to name the most obvious demographic markers. Such samples are usually referred to as *probability samples.* Because we relied on respondents who were members of volunteer survey panels, we could not control who chose to take part in our survey. Thus our responses do not reflect exactly the demographics of the populations we were sampling, and our samples are technically not probability samples.

This is a common occurrence in surveys that is typically handled by *weighting,* or propensity scoring, a process by which survey responses are adjusted upward or downward to match the actual demographic variable of interest. Weighting is often based on population data from the U.S. Census Bureau. For instance, if there were only 25 women in a sample of 100 people and we were interested in comparing the answers of women and men, the value of women's responses would be adjusted upward to reflect their true proportion in the population, slightly more than 50 percent in the United States; the men's responses would be adjusted downward. Because most leading market research firms use pre-recruited panels, post-survey weighting is almost always necessary.

There are several aspects of our survey method that might affect generalizability. First, because our survey required respondents to have Internet access, we could not include people who did not have access. Currently, about 73 percent of American adults report having regular access to the Internet (Madden, 2006). The number of teen users is higher, 87 percent in 2005 (Lenhart et al., 2005). We recognize that people who do not have Internet access might have different views about engineering than those who do have access.

A second aspect of our survey method that might affect generalizability involves the participation of minorities in general-population surveys. Minorities have traditionally been less likely to respond to sample surveys. Factors that may explain their underrepresentation include disengagement from the issues, lower levels of literacy, and inadequate contact information, which makes it less likely that they will be included in sampling frames (Sheldon et al., 2007). Although the minority gap is closing (Crocket and Ante, 2007), it remains a problem for survey researchers.

Because one of our major goals is to develop messages that target traditionally underrepresented groups, we adopted a two-step approach to overcoming the minority gap. The first step was to conduct an initial survey of the age groups of interest. Not surprisingly, African Americans and other minorities were underrepresented in this sample, as compared to the general population.

We, therefore, secured funding to field our survey in oversamples of African American and Hispanic respondents. The additional samples provided us with comparison groups to the general population. There were enough respondents in each group to make statistically valid inferences.

A third issue that may have affected generalizability was that NAE was identified as the sponsor of the research in the materials provided to survey respondents at the beginning of the questionnaire. This was necessary for securing fully informed consent from respondents, but it may also have influenced the responses to one or more questions. All of our results are interpreted with this caveat in mind.

Finally, in any survey, some people choose not to participate. The reasons for non-responses vary but can include disinterest in or aversion to the survey topic or discomfort with the survey methodology (e.g., keyboarding in an Internet-based survey). Because non-responses change the representativeness of a sample, the rate of non-response can affect generalizability. Some surveys—but not ours—try to correct for non-responses by contacting non-responders outside of the survey process to determine their reasons for not participating. Couper (2000) provides a good overview of this and other issues related to Web-based surveys.

DEVELOPMENT OF A POSITIONING STATEMENT, THEMES, AND MESSAGES

Ad hoc attempts by engineering organizations and others to promote a positive image of engineering, although well intentioned, have often fallen short, in part because most of the promoters do not have the knowledge or experience necessary to develop, test, and disseminate effective messages. A key premise for this project, therefore, is that the engineering community—and the committee itself—would benefit by involving communications and market-research professionals.

To find the best match between this project and a professional communications/marketing firm to carry out research, the National Academy of Engineering (NAE) developed a request for proposals (RFP) and posted a downloadable version on the NAE website in early April 2006. Notice of the solicitation was disseminated to approximately 100 market-research firms via the Researcher Sourcebook Directory (on the website for Quirk's Marketing Research Review, *www.quirks.com*). An additional 20 research and communications firms identified by a consultant to the project were notified directly. The maximum acceptable bid was set at $100,000, in keeping with the terms of the original proposal to the National Science Foundation (NSF).

Project staff conducted an initial screening of the 15 responses to the RFP to assess the qualifications of the responding organizations. The screening criteria related to the completeness of company descriptive information, appropriateness of the plan and personnel to carry out the research, relevant past work, and pricing information. Six of the 15 met enough of the evaluation criteria to advance to a second round of review, this time by the project committee, which conducted in-person interviews and then made a selection—the team of Bemporad Baranowski Marketing Group (BBMG; *www.bbmg.com*), a communications firm, and Global Strategy Group (GSG; *www.globalstrategygroup. com*), a market research company.

COMMUNICATIONS AUDIT

Developing a vision for new messages requires knowledge of past and current efforts. With that in mind, BBMG and GSG (BBMG/GSG) conducted a communications "audit," a wide-ranging review of previous messaging research (e.g., Davis and Gibbin, 2002; EWEP, 2005; Harris Interactive, 2004, 2006) and the kinds of communications materials that were being used to promote engineering in the public arena (e.g., by National Engineers Week, *www.eweek.org*). The results of the audit, described below, were discussed with the project committee and used to inform plans for qualitative and quantitative research.

The audit confirmed much of what had been reported in *Raising Public Awareness of Engineering* (NAE, 2002).

- **Ad hoc efforts.** Up to now, engineering outreach and message development have been mostly ad hoc. Few organizations or communicators have used written strategic communications plans.
- **Scant data on outcomes.** Measuring outcomes has been difficult, largely because of the ad hoc nature of current efforts. Very few organizations have used metrics that produce results that can be tracked, although most of them believe their programs are successful.

- **Lack of coordination.** Outreach efforts have been poorly coordinated or not coordinated at all. Nevertheless, there is a strong desire in the engineering community for a coordinated campaign, especially in terms of communicating the contributions of engineering to people's welfare and the career benefits of engineering. However, coordination has been stymied by lack of clear leadership, limited resources, and inadequate infrastructure.
- **Few attempts to reach youngsters.** Most outreach initiatives have targeted older students (i.e., high school students) in an effort to prime the engineering education "pipeline." Less attention has been paid to elementary and middle school students, when stimulating interest in engineering might also serve a "mainline" function, namely promoting technological literacy and increasing interest in mathematics and science.
- **Local outreach.** With a few exceptions, notably National Engineers Week, most outreach programs have been local. National Engineers Week is considered one of the most effective outreach efforts, although no data have been collected showing changes in student attitudes about engineering or interest in pursuing engineering as a career.
- **Diverse approaches.** Engineering outreach efforts have used a variety of tactics and approaches, including design-and-build competitions, mentoring programs, and tool kits for teachers and guidance counselors. This wide variety of activities has made it difficult to deliver a consistent message and contributed to inconsistent messages, even from a single organization.

In general, messages targeting younger children attempt to convince them that mathematics and science are easy and fun and that engineering is challenging, exciting, hands-on, and rewarding work. Encouragement ("You can do it!") is a common undercurrent. Messages for older, prospective college students tend to reinforce the excitement and rewards of an engineering career (engineering prepares you for success and gives you opportunities to use your knowledge in creative ways that will improve people's lives). For the most part, messages that promote engineering have been direct, rational statements emphasizing the *benefits* of engineering. Typical messages for students include:

- An engineering education is a sound basis for a career.
- Engineering offers challenges, excitement, opportunities, and satisfaction.
- Engineering is worthwhile, challenging, fun, and within reach.

A second recurring theme has been to link engineering to *skills* in mathematics and science. These messages frequently suggest that students must have a high aptitude and strong interest in these subjects to succeed in engineering.

As part of information gathering for a planned larger messaging effort (ultimately funded by NSF and described in this report) NAE in April 2005 brought together several advertising and public relations (PR) professionals with decades of experience in engineering or technology-related campaigns to discuss current and past messaging. This small focus group, funded by the S.D. Bechtel, Jr. Foundation, recommended that certain kinds of messages be avoided:

- *Math and science are fun or easy.* The challenge of studying math and science should not be trivialized, because engineering does require proficiency in these subjects.
- *Engineers improve the quality of life.* This message is not unique to engineers and may not be readily believable.
- *Engineers design and build things.* Although this is what engineers do, the message does not do justice to the importance of engineering.

At the end of the discussion, the group identified the following categories for the development of messages:

- *Engineers are necessary.* Emphasize the critical importance of engineering accomplishments.

- *Engineers have answers.* If not, they are the ones who can find answers.
- *Engineers/engineering make(s) things happen or make(s) things better.*
- *Engineers connect things.* Engineers link creativity and practicality.

The BBMG/GSG audit also reviewed a message-development project undertaken by the Extraordinary Women Engineers Project (EWEP). From June 2004 to January 2005, EWEP conducted focus groups, online and in person, as well as surveys of high school girls, teachers, and school counselors; engineering students; and professional engineers (EWEP, 2005). The goal of the project was to determine girls' perceptions of engineering and the perceptions of the people who influence them. The overarching conclusion of the project was bleak (EWEP, 2005):

> High school girls believe engineering is for people who love both math and science. They do not have an understanding of what engineering is. They do not show an interest in the field, nor …think it is 'for them.'

The report went on to note a disconnect between the messages being conveyed by the engineering community and the key career and academic motivators for girls (Figure 2-1).

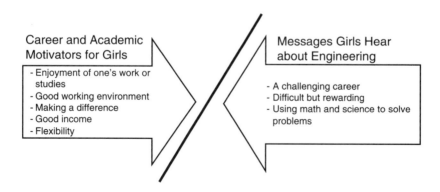

FIGURE 2-1 Differences between known motivators for career choices by girls and messages from the engineering community.

REFRAMING THE IMAGE OF ENGINEERING

Based on the communications audit and discussions with the committee, BBMG/GSG advised us to reframe the way engineering and engineers are presented to the public. They recommended that we stop talking about engineering primarily in terms of benefits to the individual and required skills and focus instead on ideas and impact.

Strategic Elements of an Effective Message

Make It Personal

To bring the experience of engineering to life, the message should ascribe authentic, vibrant personality traits to *engineers*. Engineers themselves should be central to the reframed image of engineering. They work with people, not abstract fields of study or career pursuits.

The message should include humor, wit, and irony to convey a human quality to the tone and voice behind the message. Messages that break through the clutter must make an emotional connection with their audiences, especially a young audience. The message should use *their* language, not impose *our* language. Language and word choices have a direct bearing on the emotional appeal of a message.

Show, Don't Tell

From a marketing perspective, labeling something as "cool" sounds a death knell, especially when kids and teens are the targets. Messages should be evocative rather than didactic. They should use metaphors, analogies, and symbols whenever possible. Messages should be embedded in stories that dramatize the rich legacy of engineering achievements.

Engineering messages can be effective on television because engineering lends itself to visual images. Yet, most current images reinforce the stale, one-dimensional image of engineers as operators and builders. At some point, a robust visual inventory should be developed and a serious investment made in developing an updated gallery of images.

Find "Campaignable" Ideas

Given the diverse activities and careers encompassed in engineering, testing *campaignable* ideas was essential during the research phase of the project. A campaignable idea is derived from an overarching theme with enough emotional relevance and power to connect a broad range of specific messages. It represents a unifying concept, the tip of the iceberg, and gains traction by virtue of a strategic, integrated marketing and communications effort and enough time and resources to move the needle of public awareness and change attitudes. Campaignable ideas can be readily adapted to appeal to different audiences and meet different needs.[1]

Find (and Mind) the Perception Gap

Perhaps the most important prerequisite for reframing the image of engineering is having a clear understanding of the perception gap we are trying to close. To communicate the unique values of engineering, our consultants recommended we shift negative perceptions to more positive ones (Table 2-1).

DEVELOPING A POSITIONING STATEMENT

Behind every powerful brand is a positioning statement that serves as a compass or guideline, pointing the way to the development of a robust communications program. As a guide to changing the perception of engineering from a profession that yields personal *benefits* and requires certain *skills* to a profession based on creative *ideas* that have a beneficial *impact*, BBMG/GSG developed, and the committee endorsed, the following positioning statement (Box 2-1):

---

[1]Several recent campaigns have shown that seemingly fragmented industries, in which coordination seemed a distant reality, can rebrand themselves and cultivate new identities that shift public perceptions. A few examples of successful industry rebranding campaigns include cotton ("The fabric of our lives."; *www.thefabricofourlives.com*), milk ("Got milk?"; *www.bodybymilk.com*), beef ("It's what's for dinner."; *www.beefitswhatsfordinner.com*), and pork ("The other white meat."; *www.theotherwhitemeat.com*).

TABLE 2-1 Suggestions for Changing the Perceptions of Engineering

From Current Perceptions	To New, More Positive Perceptions
Builders, operators, planners, and maintainers	Designers, creators, and inventors
Computer people	Many types of engineers
Geeks and nerds	Creative professionals, "imagineers"
White males	People of all backgrounds
Boring	Dynamic and exciting work that makes a difference
Too difficult to learn	Challenging but worth the effort
A man's job	Engineering is a field for men and women
Not as prestigious as a scientist	A prestigious job that helps make the world a better place
Less lucrative than law or medicine	Supports a very comfortable lifestyle

---

BOX 2-1
A Positioning Statement for Engineering

No profession unleashes the spirit of innovation like engineering. From research to real-world applications, engineers constantly discover how to improve our lives by creating bold new solutions that connect science to life in unexpected, forward-thinking ways. Few professions turn so many ideas into so many realities. Few have such a direct and positive effect on people's everyday lives. We are counting on engineers and their imaginations to help us meet the needs of the 21st century.

A strong positioning statement like this one is necessary for several reasons. First, it is a point of reference for all public communications (e.g., advertising, PR campaigns). Second, it encourages a consistent message (i.e., staying on message). Third, it clarifies the aspects of engineering that set it apart from other professions. Fourth, it makes a clear case for why engineering matters.

As noted in Chapter 1, a positioning statement is the conceptual foundation for a communications campaign, but it is not usually shared with the public. However, even though the text of a positioning statement never appears in external communications, all messages and taglines are directly linked to it.

In Chapter 1, we pointed out that positioning statements answer a number of core questions about the "brand." Here is how the proposed statement aligns with those questions:

> No profession unleashes the spirit of innovation like engineering *(who)*. From research to real-world applications *(what business)*, engineers constantly discover how to improve our lives *(special needs)* by creating bold new solutions that connect science to life in unexpected, forward-thinking ways *(unique benefit)*. Few professions *(competitors)* turn so many ideas into so many realities *(the difference)*. Few have such a direct and positive effect on people's everyday lives. We *(who served)* are counting on engineers and their imaginations to help us meet the needs of the 21st century.

Preliminary Themes and Messages

Guided by the positioning statement, in consultation with the committee, BBMG/GSG proposed six preliminary themes and sample messages—three focused on engineers and three on the engineering profession. The messages were later refined based on qualitative research (i.e., focus groups and triads), the next phase of the project (described in Chapter 3).

Themes/Messages Focused on Engineers

Limitless Imagination
- Engineers are "imagineers." They see possibilities. They dream about making things better.
- Engineers are curious. They ask questions, "How does it work?", "Where does it go?", "What will happen if?"
- Engineers are creative problem-solvers. Like artists, engineers have a vision of how something should work, and they are passionate about that vision.
- It takes teamwork to bring creative ideas to life. Engineers work with other smart, imaginative people, such as animators, architects, astronomers, chemists, physicians, meteorologists, and physicists, to design and create new things.

Enterprising Spirit
- Engineers like to invent things. They create new products, imagine new gadgets, and launch new companies to turn their ideas into reality.
- Engineers are nimble and quick, able to think on their feet and work wonders using the tools and technologies available to them.
- Engineers understand the practical applications of their work, how it will make a difference in people's everyday lives.

Free to Explore
- Engineers love to explore and discover. They see life as a journey, a quest for better ideas. Engineers dream up smarter robots, faster sports cars, new medical devices, and ways to reduce pollution.
- Engineers think outside the box. They take things apart to see how they work. They are constantly learning new things.
- Engineers are never bored. They adventurously seek out problems that need solving. They are constantly being challenged and inspired to keep exploring.

Themes/Messages Focused on Engineering

Ideas in Action
- Engineering bridges the world of science and the real world. It turns ideas into reality.
- From the grandest skyscrapers to microscopic medical devices, engineering plays a role in almost everything we experience.
- Engineering is on the cutting edge. Engineers use the latest science, tools, and technologies to advance society and improve people's lives.

Shape the Future
- Knowing how to turn dreams into reality is totally empowering. It's a skill that lasts a lifetime.
- As an engineer, you can shape your future and the world's future. You can help solve tomorrow's problems today.

- Engineering offers many lucrative career options in research, development, design, construction, sales, and management. It's worth the hard work it takes to become an engineer.
- Engineers say that seeing their ideas come to life, having a direct effect on people's everyday lives, is far and away the most rewarding aspect of the job.

Life Takes Engineering
- Engineering could not be more relevant. Our society is becoming increasingly complex. We must provide more food and energy for a rapidly growing population, and we must limit damage to the environment in the process. Engineering will play a big role in meeting these challenges.
- Engineering is good for our economy. It's big business, and it provides millions of jobs. It makes this country stronger, safer, and more competitive.
- Engineering makes a world of difference. From new medical equipment and safer drinking water to faster microchips, engineers apply their knowledge to improve people's lives in concrete, meaningful ways.

Each of these messages and themes can be traced back to the positioning statement. For example, the "Limitless Imagination" theme describes engineers as curious and visionary, as creative problem-solvers who want to make things better. This connects to the description in the positioning statement of engineers as focused on discovery, innovation, and creative solutions. The "Ideas into Action" theme suggests that engineering is a bridge between the world of science and the real world and is responsible for the technological improvements we enjoy. This theme connects to the notion of engineers turning ideas into reality, with direct, positive effects on people's lives.

CONCLUSION

The communications audit conducted by BBMG/GSG identified recurring themes in current messaging and collected useful, although limited, data on what adults and teens think about the engineering profession. Through an iterative process between the consultants and the committee a new more powerful vision of engineering emerged and was encapsulated in a positioning statement (Box 2-1). Several themes and messages based on that statement were developed by BBMG/GSG in consultation with the committee.

Positioning statements are the core of successful marketing campaigns. In the case of engineering, the proposed positioning statement represents a dramatic shift in point of view. The focus is no longer on required skills and personal benefits. Instead, the emphasis is on the connection between engineering and ideas and possibilities.

The new statement is an optimistic, aspirational expression of a field that has, up until now, been portrayed in much more pedestrian terms—a math- and science-dependent process for solving problems. Engineering is that, of course, but it is also much more. It is inherently creative, concerned with human welfare, and an emotionally satisfying calling. In short, the new positioning statement changes the conversation about engineering.

REFERENCES

Davis, L., and R. Gibbin. 2002. Raising Public Awareness of Engineering. Washington, D.C.: The National Academies Press.

EWEP (Extraordinary Women Engineers Project). 2005. Extraordinary Women Engineers—Final Report, April 2005. Available online at *http://www.eweek.org/site/news/Eweek/EWE_Needs_Asses.pdf.* (July 16, 2007)

Harris Interactive. 2004. American Perspectives on Engineers and Engineering. Poll conducted for the American Association of Engineering Societies. Final report, February 13, 2004. Available online at *http://www.aaes.org/harris_2004_files/frame.htm.* (July 6, 2007)

Harris Interactive. 2006. Firefighters, doctors and nurses top list as "most prestigious occupations," according to latest Harris poll. *The Harris Poll®* #58, July 26, 2006. Available online at *http://www.harrisinteractive.com/harris_poll/index.asp?PID=685.* (July 6, 2007)

NAE (National Academy of Engineering). 2002. Raising Public Awareness of Engineering. L. Davis and R. Gibbin, eds. Washington, D.C.: The National Academies Press.

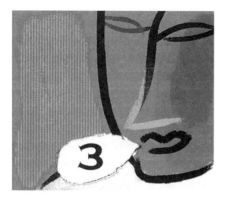

RESEARCH
RESULTS

The communications audit provided a comprehensive overview and critique of the strategic approaches and tactics used to date to communicate with the public about engineering. Combined with input from the committee, the audit gave the consultants a solid basis on which to develop a positioning statement and preliminary themes and messages. The consultants then conducted qualitative and quantitative research, which added to our knowledge of stakeholder perceptions of engineering, vetted preliminary messages, validated the positioning statement, and provided an evidence base for recommendations.

The qualitative research comprised individual interviews, adult and teen focus groups, and "triads" (groups of three) with preteens. The quantitative research consisted of an online survey. Consistent with federal rules for research on human subjects, the National Academy of Engineering established procedures, including informed consent, to ensure the confidentiality of research participants. This process was overseen by the National Academies Institutional Review Board.

QUALITATIVE RESEARCH

Qualitative research involving small samples selected without using statistical procedures must be considered exploratory, and the resulting hypotheses may have to be validated by quantitative research. Qualitative research can sometimes provide clear conclusions but is designed primarily to shed light on perceptions of the issues in question, in this case engineering and engineers.

In-Depth Interviews

In the first phase of the qualitative research for this study (September and October 2006), Bemporad Baranowski Marketing Group/ Global Srategy Group (BBMG/GSG) conducted 12 in-depth interviews of a cross section of educators, opinion leaders, and engineers. By talking with individuals familiar with engineering, BBMG/GSG hoped to confirm and build on the conclusions of the communications audit and discussions with the committee. The interviewees were the first group outside of the committee to weigh in on the messages and themes.

Methodology

The interviews were conducted by telephone and tape recorded to ensure that they were reported accurately. Each interview lasted 45 minutes to an hour. (An interviewer's guide can be viewed at Appendix B.) The project committee and staff suggested potential interviewees, but BBMG/GSG made the final selection. In keeping with the informed-consent process, the identities of the interviewees were not revealed to the committee or project staff.

Key Findings

Perceptions of Engineers and Engineering. The interviews revealed a wide gap between the way engineers would like themselves and their field to be perceived and the way both are actually perceived. At best, engineers are seen—and see themselves—as curious, hard-working individuals who design solutions to difficult problems and leave their mark on the world. As the chair of a university chemical engineering department said, "They [engineers] are the interface between society and technology."

However, engineers can also be very hard on themselves. Sometimes they describe themselves and others in engineering as "Dilberts", that is, "book smart," "nerdy" "know-it-alls" who are "isolated," "myopic," and "not cool." Some argue that this stereotype is unfair and have criticized their peers for not doing a better job of explaining exactly what engineers do. As a researcher in a corporate research and developoment division said, "Engineers are seen as nerds and geeks. People who are not in it [the field] have a hard time grasping what we do, [and] we don't do a good job of explaining it either. It [engineering] is seen as a bunch of technical things they can't grasp . . . and boring, too."

Many interviewees noted that there is no readily identifiable "public face" of engineering, no personality, such as Julia Child for cooking, Oprah Winfrey for talk television, Tiger Woods for golf, or Martha Stewart for home living. Some felt that cable TV programs that explain "the way things work" or feature engineering "marvels" expose many more people to a positive image of the field than the best-organized "engineering fair" or "popsicle-stick bridge-building contest," which only attract people who are already interested in engineering.

Interviewees who are engineers expressed concerns that the contributions of engineering to everyday lives are taken for granted. To an observant eye, engineering is all around us, but it takes a "powerful awareness" to be able to see it. A columnist for a major newspaper said, "Engineering is the behind-the-scenes job that no one pays attention to, and it doesn't have to be that way."

Several interviewees said that the lack of diversity in engineering is a significant issue. "If anything, I'd like to make it [engineering] more appealing for minorities and women," said a Ph.D. candidate and member of the National Society of Black Engineers. As noted in Chapter 1, women and some minorities are significantly underrepresented in engineering education and practice.

One reason for the difficulty in communicating effectively with the public is that the technical aspects of engineering—especially mathematics and science, which are perceived as difficult—are usually emphasized, rather than the creative opportunities. As a vocational instructor and middle school technology teacher explained, "Students don't …understand that [engineering] is really a super-creative job. They don't see that [engineers] are probably more artistic than some artists. [Engineers] are just using a different set of paints, if you will."

Reactions to Messages. All of the preliminary messages and themes (Box 3-1) were well received, except for "An Enterprising Spirit" and "Free to Explore." Both engineers and educators embraced the image of engineering as creative, imaginative problem-solving and overcoming "seeming impossibilities."

Focus Groups and Youth Triads

In mid-October 2006, BBMG/GSG conducted four focus groups with young people ages 12 to 15 and 16 to 19 (one in each age group in Raleigh, North Carolina, and in Phoenix, Arizona) and a single focus group with parents of young people ages 9 to 19 in Raleigh. BBMG/GSG also conducted four same-sex youth triads with children ages 9 to 11 in Phoenix.[1]

The purpose of the focus groups and triads was to explore teens and children's understanding of engineering, their impressions of engineers, and their reactions to examples of engineering and messages about engineering. In addition, the student groups were asked their opinions on current school subjects and their ideas about future careers. The parent group was asked what they thought was important in career choices for their children.

---

[1]One-on-one interviews with young children are notorious for causing respondents to "shut down," and focus groups with young children are similarly unproductive. In triads, the three friends already have a rapport and are accustomed to playing and talking with each other. All qualitative methods will introduce some bias, and with triads there may be a "pecking order" effect. GSG has conducted youth triads with great success for such clients as the Boy Scouts and Scholastic.

BOX 3-1
Reactions to Preliminary Messages, Selected Quotes

Ideas in Action (underscores that engineering bridges the world of science and the real world).

> "That's what engineering does. That's what got me into engineering. I didn't want to go into chemistry. I thought engineering was more practical."
>
> Chemical engineer, international industrial gas company

Life Takes Engineering (focuses on the life-changing work of engineers).

> "No kidding. Life does take engineering. [The word] *life* adds depth to the subject. It speaks to people on all levels. It speaks to people who aren't as fortunate [as we] to have the greatest environment to live in. It gives them aspirations for greatness. It's changing your life for the better."
>
> Vocational instructor and middle school technology teacher

Limitless Imagination (focuses on the innovative nature of engineering design).

> "Creative ideas often lead to elegant solutions, like the Segway."
>
> Computer architect, major semiconductor company

Free to Explore (evokes the constant journey, the engineer's quest for new solutions).

> "Is that always true? Is it always a new solution you're looking for, or is it to take existing solutions and apply them in certain circumstances?"
>
> Columnist, major newspaper

Shape the Future (engineering as an empowering, rewarding career).

> "You're talking about making a difference in so many ways: from artificial limbs to XBox 360."
>
> Ph.D. candidate, National Society of Black Engineers

An Enterprising Spirit (the inventive spirit and pioneering contributions of engineering).

> "[The word] *enterprising* conveys much more of a business aspect, and kids won't understand that until later. It gives a business flavor, so I'm not sure about that one."
>
> Planner, NASA

Methodology

Focus group respondents were recruited by telephone by professional recruiters calling from a residential telephone list. Respondents were eligible only if they had not participated in a market research group discussion, focus group, or individual interview in the previous six months. Adult participants were parents of children in school ages 9 to 19 who were "planning to attend or . . . currently attending college." Adult respondents were informed that the project consisted of an informal discussion group "to learn more about how parents feel regarding various issues that impact their child's education and career choices." All teen respondents were currently "planning to attend or . . . currently attending college." Teens were informed by recruiters that the discussion groups were being conducted "to learn more about how young people feel about their education and career choices." Teens ages 16–18 were eligible to participate only if they had not already chosen to pursue a specific, non-science-related career, or if they might change their mind about a chosen career. Teens were also asked for their opinions about several possible professions or career choices they may choose, and asked if they thought that profession or career choice would be a very good choice, a good choice, a fair choice, or a bad choice for them. Teen respondents were ineligible to participate if they believed engineering was a "bad choice" for them, personally.

A total of 28 teens, 12 pre-teens, and 10 adults participated in the focus groups and triads. According to demographic data collected by BBMG/GSG, between 20 and 50 percent of individuals in each focus group considered themselves minority (i.e., non white). Participants were recruited and screened by local research firms selected by the consultants, and the sessions were held at the facilities of the local firms in rooms with one-way mirrors, which enabled consultants and project staff to observe the discussions without distracting the participants. Committee members and project staff who were not onsite were able to observe the sessions in Phoenix via video on a password-protected website.

The focus sessions lasted about two hours and were professionally moderated according to committee-approved discussion guides (see Appendixes C and D). Participants received a small financial incentive and were required to sign informed-consent forms.

Triads lasted from 45 minutes to an hour, and moderators again used a committee-approved discussion guide (Appendix E). Like the focus groups, the triads were held in rooms with one-way mirrors. The general format was the same as for the teen and adult focus groups, with one exception. Children were asked to react to engineering-related pictures rather than to respond to the message themes directly. Parents signed consent forms on behalf of their minor children.

Findings

Perceptions of Engineers and Engineering. Students struggling to understand the concept of engineering—especially younger children and older children with little interest in math, science, or computer games—connected the word "engineering" to the word "engine" and thus concluded it had something to do with vehicles, such as cars, trains, and army tanks. One Phoenix teen in the 12–15-year-old group thought engineering must be "being able to fix things that are part of the engine."

Other researchers have also found that children have a relatively narrow idea of engineering (Cunningham et al., 2005). The majority of students understood that engineers "design and build things" but tended to have a very limited idea of what that meant, focusing mainly on mechanical or structural aspects of engineering, like cars, bridges, and buildings. One teen in Raleigh had a more comprehensive view. Engineering, he said, is about "designing buildings, making blueprints, making stuff work . . .Taking things apart and putting them back together better, like electronics . . . Making new products that are more efficient, like a trash can that can go to the curb by itself."

When the moderators explained (via written examples for the teen groups and pictures for the preteens) that engineering is all around us, the students became much more interested in engineering as a possible field of study. The examples helped them understand the broad reach of engineering, how it benefits society, and how it might be connected to something that interests them. "If you told somebody that they could invent the next Xbox, you'd get a lot of kids who'd want to be an engineer," declared a teen in the 12–15-year-old focus group in Phoenix.

Students who were most aware of engineering—older children, particularly if they had a parent or family friend or relative who was an engineer, and students who already had a strong interest in science and math—included computers and technology, space exploration, traffic and city planning, and other topics in their definitions. Even these students, however, were not sure of the role of engineering in actual projects. In fact, even the few students who said they planned to become engineers had little understanding of the kinds of tasks involved in performing a job or pursuing a career.

When asked to describe the qualities of engineers, students tended to emphasize that engineers were "smart," "imaginative," and good at math and science when they were kids. Although they did not have a negative impression of engineers, many seemed to feel that they themselves were not smart enough or did not enjoy math or science enough to become engineers. One preteen commented, "Certain kids can become engineers. If dumb kids try to become engineers, it isn't going to work well. [Engineering is for] smart kids who know how to fix things . . . For cars, you need to know math and science, how this plus this equals mileage."

If some students thought that engineers were smart, creative, and imaginative, many others thought they were sedentary, worked mostly on computers, and had little contact with other people. "Seems like a lot of engineers sit behind a desk and don't do much field work," said one Raleigh teen in the 16–19-year-old group. "It's a desk job. I'd beat my head against the wall if I had to do that . . . When you think of engineering, you don't think about being in front of people."

Nearly all of the girls who took part in the research said they thought women could be engineers as well as men. However, there was a strong underlying assumption that girls "who like things that boys tend to like" (e.g., video games, cars and vehicles, building things) were more likely to become engineers than "average girls" (e.g., girls who want to be veterinarians, lawyers, doctors, fashion designers, teachers, or otherwise want to "work with people").

When asked to name engineers they knew or had heard of, including those who had visited their schools on career days, most students could name only men. Almost everyone—students and parents of both genders—agreed that no concerted efforts had been made to engage women in engineering or to demonstrate to girls how science, math, and engineering are related to the things they are most likely to care about.

Examples of Engineering. Students were asked to review a list of examples of engineering (Table 3-1) (for focus groups) or pictures of engineering-related artifacts or people engaged in activities (for triads) and pick the examples they found most interesting or appealing. The results showed that students tended to pick examples of the things they "connect with" personally. This suggests that a broad variety of examples would appeal to a very wide range of children, as long as the examples include concepts related to students' interests.

TABLE 3-1 Examples of Engineering Shown to Students in Focus Groups

- How the pyramids were built
- Space
- Designing video games
- Building an acoustically perfect concert hall
- What makes a bridge
- Building the world's tallest bridge (over 1,000 feet high)
- Designing the world's fastest plane
- Developing new foods
- How MRI machines work
- DNA testing
- Using DNA evidence to solve crimes
- Cars that run on alternative fuels
- Making cars safer
- Growing organs for emergency transplants
- Making smaller, faster computer processors
- Protecting the rainforest
- High-speed (250 mph) trains
- Developing new fabrics
- Automotive design
- Computer-aided design
- Missile defense systems
- Interactive television
- Traffic design
- High-definition television
- Nuclear fission
- Internet security systems
- iPod
- Making homes safer
- How a million Twinkies are made every day
- How tower cranes work
- Velcro
- High-speed image transmission
- High-performance racing cars
- Turning deserts into farmland
- Wind power
- Solar energy
- Machines that allow blind people to see

Examples of objects and activities children were familiar with in their daily lives stimulated the most interest. For example, students repeatedly expressed enthusiasm for video games, iPods, computers, cell phones, and amusement parks. High-tech devices, such as the iPod and video games, were picked by a broad range of children, while pictures of the microchip were picked mostly by science- and math-oriented students. Some students found images and descriptions of space exploration interesting, while others gravitated more toward historical examples of engineering (e.g., catapults or pyramids).

Younger girls tended to pick images that showed people, particularly older female engineers, while boys were more likely to pick images that featured "things." This finding is consistent with other research on thing–people orientation among girls and boys (e.g., Lippa, 1998). Many older girls seemed to gravitate toward "DNA evidence" from the list of examples. Young students did not select pictures of individuals standing still or sitting at a desk, which reflected their image of engineering as "boring or repetitive" and "not with other people."

Reactions to Message Themes. Students generally reacted positively to the message themes. They especially liked descriptions of engineers as "creative problem solvers" and "free to explore." The creative aspect of engineering "grabbed me," said one Raleigh 16–19-year old. "[T]hat appeals to me a lot more than trying to describe them as scientists . . . The never-ending part appeals to me . . . there's so much you can do with [engineering]." One Raleigh 12–15-year-old student liked the theme suggesting "that you'll never be bored. Keeping interest is the best thing in a job . . . Makes it sound like an adventure . . . something I wouldn't mind sitting through two calculus courses for."

Students expressed a very strong sense of the importance of choosing careers that will provide financial stability and a comfortable lifestyle. The career goal named most often was "making good money." Another concept that had strong appeal as a career goal was "helping to make a difference." However, many students found it difficult to connect engineering and helping others.

Most students thought that engineers might make a difference, but only *indirectly*, whereas doctors and lawyers, who have direct contact with others, have a more obvious impact on people. "Engineering is behind the scenes helping people," observed a 16–19-year-old Raleigh student. "They design the machines that help people. You don't think of an engineer when you see a building or machine, you think that is a great machine. But when a doctor does something, you know that they did it."

This perception may explain why very few students associated major engineering challenges for the next generation (e.g., "cars that will help us achieve oil independence" or "saving the rainforest") with "making a difference." Several students also hinted that a career in engineering might not fulfill their desire for recognition. This idea was based on a conception that engineers draw more satisfaction from individual or team-oriented work than from direct recognition or the gratitude of users or beneficiaries.

Parents. Most parents said that engineering would be a good field for their children to consider. Even those who were not certain about what engineers do were confident that engineering would provide job security—a top priority for parents—in the form of good salary and benefits, as well as a career path for advancement and success. "You can test waters in different disciplines within engineering. It is a good career choice," said one parent.

Parents had a mixed perception of engineers, however. On the one hand, they saw them as very smart problem solvers whose work is critical to society. On the other hand, they perceived them as somewhat nerdy and, perhaps, too focused on understanding how things work or trying to make things more efficient. As one parent said, "I think it is a certain personality type. I know it is a stereotype, but I think [engineers] tend to see things more black and white....Very precise, detail oriented, they are not going to get into a conversation about politics or news."

In the discussion of message themes, parents tended to prefer the practical messages, underscoring their interest in job security for their children. They strongly agreed that "creative problem solving," "freedom to explore," and "making a difference" would appeal to their kids, but they were more intent on making sure their kids find a career that will keep them financially secure. "Tell them to find something that is reasonably satisfying and you can make a living at," counseled one parent.

QUANTITATIVE RESEARCH

Once the information provided from the communications audit and qualitative research had been digested, the committee moved to obtain quantitative data, which are important for at least two reasons. First, they provide a check on the findings and interpretations of the qualitative research. Second, they provide a statistically sound foundation for making a case for new messaging to present to the engineering community.

Methodology

The online survey was administered in two phases: to an initial sample of teens and adults in December 2006 and two oversamples of African American and Hispanic teens and adults in spring 2007. The survey instrument (Appendix F), which was developed by BBMG/GSG in an iterative process with the committee, included six questions about views of engineering and engineers and four questions about reactions to messages and taglines. Some of these questions asked respondents to rate or choose among multiple answers. To avoid the possibility that the choices at or near the top or at or near the bottom of the list would be preferentially selected (so-called order effect), the order of answers was randomized for each respondent.

Adults in all three samples were asked about their level of interest in the news and engagement in the community. This information was used to create a category of "informed adults," individuals with some college education who said they either followed the news on an ongoing basis, including local, state, and national political developments, or were involved in their communities as volunteers.

For the initial sample, GSG fielded the questionnaire in a panel recruited by Polimetrix (*www.polimetrix.com*). The survey was completed by 1,234 individuals, 666 adults (including an oversample of 200 informed adults) and 568 teens, ages 14 to 17. As noted in Chapter 1, there were relatively few African Americans and Hispanics in the initial sample (only 77 non-white adults and 116 non-white teens); thus, statistically speaking, it was impossible to draw valid conclusions about the responses of these groups.

Because African Americans and Hispanics are a key audience for engineering messaging, the committee decided to enlarge the survey sample to include these populations. The oversampling was conducted in late May and early June 2007 by Harris Interactive (*www. harrisinteractive.com*) and returned 605 surveys from African American adults, 608 surveys from Hispanic adults, 535 surveys from African American teens, and 566 surveys from Hispanic teens. Like BBMG/ GSG, Harris Interactive relied on pre-recruited panels of respondents. All survey samples were statistically weighted to adjust for potential demographic differences between the final sample and the general population.

When interpreting the results of the online survey, it is important to keep in mind that data for the initial and African American and Hispanic samples were obtained at different times and data were collected differently. Although every effort was made to ensure that the wording and order of the questions were the same for all the samples, other variables, such as the visual presentation, could not be as easily controlled. In other words, the mode of data collection may have influenced responses.

For this reason, the committee's analysis is focused on relative rankings *within* each sample, rather than potentially misleading differences *among* samples. The ranking numbers (in parentheses) in the tables that follow should be interpreted cautiously, because when the point spread between two percentages was smaller than the sampling tolerance,[2] it was impossible to determine relative rankings of the responses.

---

[2]The sampling tolerances for comparing adult and teen samples and for comparing gender samples ranges from 4 to 10 percent, depending on the survey response percentages and the sizes of the samples. In the tables that follow, the committee has shaded data for which the differences exceeded the sampling tolerances.

Assuring Socioeconomic, Educational, and Geographical Representativeness

Surveys such as ours need to be sensitive to the diversity of the U.S. population, because people from diverse backgrounds may not share the same views on engineering. For this reason, both GSG and Harris sought participation of teens and adults from a range of income, educational, and geographic backgrounds. As a result, our data reflect input from important subpopulations, such as those of low income and limited education, and those living in rural regions of the country.

For example, income information collected in the two Harris surveys revealed 28 percent of African American adults and 34 percent of Hispanic adults had household income below the 2006 median for their race or ethnicity, $31,969 and $37,781, respectively (DeNavas-Walt et al., 2007). In 2006, median household income for white Americans was $50,673 and for all races it was $48,201.

No income data were requested of adults in the initial sample. However, it is possible to use information about educational attainment to estimate a person's socioeconomic status. In the initial sample, 39 percent of adults said they had no education beyond high school, and an additional 6 percent indicated they had not graduated high school. Median household income in 2005 for "householders" with no high school diploma was $24,675 and for those with no more than a high school diploma it was $38,191 (U.S. Census Bureau, 2006).

The socioeconomic status of teens in the African American and Hispanic oversamples can be estimated by their reporting of the educational attainment of their mothers and fathers. (No data regarding parental educational attainment were collected from the teens in the first survey.) These data suggest that a large minority of African American teens (between 37 and 41%) and a majority of Hispanic teens (between 52 and 57%) were from families where neither mother nor father had attended college.

Taken together, actual and inferred income data suggest that a significant proportion of adults and teens in the African American and Hispanic oversamples, and of adults in the initial sample, were of moderate to low income.

The online survey also collected geographically representative data. The initial sample and two oversamples interviewed individuals across four regions of the United States (East, Midwest, South, and West), and these data were weighted to approximate the geographical distribution of the population of the United States. In addition, Harris collected data from the two teen oversamples regarding the location of the school that respondents "currently attend or most recently attended." Approximately 50 percent of African American and Hispanic teens reported attending a school in an urban or city area; slightly more than 35 percent reported attending in a suburban area; and about 15 percent reported attending in a small town or rural area.

Perceptions of Engineering

Career Choice

When adults were asked to name a "very good choice" of career from a list of six professions, doctor, scientist, and engineer were nearly equivalent (Table 3-2). Teens put doctor at the top of the list and engineer, lawyer, or scientist second. With the exception of teens in the initial sample, teaching was at the bottom of the list.

In all of the teen samples, boys were nearly twice as likely as girls to rate engineering as a very good choice of career, and engineering was the only profession in which there was a difference between genders. This gender gap was even more dramatic in data collected by the College Board in 2006 for 1.55 million high school juniors who took the Preliminary SAT/National Merit Scholarship Qualifying Test. In those data, 14.7 percent of boys but only 2.0 percent of girls indicated they planned to major in engineering in college (College Board, 2007).

Survey takers were asked to rate the relative importance of seven factors (interesting work, availability of jobs in the field, work that makes a difference, challenging work, salary, recognition, and prestigious field) in career choices. Adults in the initial sample and Hispanic adults in the oversample rated interesting work and job availability equally as the two most important factors (Table 3-3). African American adults cited job availability as most important and interesting work second.

66

TABLE 3-2 Survey Respondents' Choices for "Very Good Choice" Careers, by Percentage (Rank)

Career	Initial Sample				African American Oversample				Hispanic Oversample			
	Adults	Teens			Adults	Teens			Adults	Teens		
		All	Boys	Girls		All	Boys	Girls		All	Boys	Girls
Engineer	56 (1)	24 (3)	34 (1)	17 (4)	58 (2)	27 (3)	36 (1)	19 (4)	61 (1)	29 (2)	39 (1)	20 (5)
Doctor	52 (2)	32 (1)	32 (3)	32 (1)	62 (1)	42 (1)	34 (2)	48 (1)	58 (2)	40 (1)	37 (2)	43 (1)
Scientist	50 (3)	*	*	*	54 (3)	23 (4)	25 (4)	22 (3)	50 (3)	22 (4)	21 (5)	23 (3)
Architect	37 (4)	17 (5)	19 (4)	16 (5)	50 (4)	19 (5)	23 (5)	16 (5)	45 (4)	20 (5)	22 (4)	17 (6)
Teacher	33 (5)	24 (3)	19 (4)	29 (2)	40 (6)	10 (6)	7 (6)	12 (6)	34 (5)	17 (6)	12 (6)	21 (4)
Lawyer	28 (6)	30 (2)	33 (2)	27 (3)	44 (5)	29 (2)	28 (3)	30 (2)	33 (6)	25 (3)	26 (3)	25 (2)

* Due to a programming error, "scientist" was not included as an answer choice for teens in the initial sample.

NOTE: Pairs of shaded cells indicate responses where differences exceeded the sampling tolerance and are therefore significant. Gray = adults vs. all teens. Black = boys vs. girls.

TABLE 3-3 Survey Respondents' Choices for "Extremely Important" Factors in Making Career Choices, Percentage (Rank)

Factor	Initial Sample				African American Oversample				Hispanic Oversample			
	Adults	Teens			Adults	Teens			Adults	Teens		
		All	Boys	Girls		All	Boys	Girls		All	Boys	Girls
Interest	48 (1)	65 (1)	63 (1)	66 (1)	50 (2)	62 (1)	59 (2)	64 (1)	49 (1)	59 (1)	56 (1)	63 (1)
Availability	48 (1)	28 (4)	32 (4)	24 (5)	61 (1)	45 (4)	42 (3)	47 (3)	48 (2)	37 (4)	36 (4)	38 (3)
Difference	41 (3)	47 (2)	45 (2)	49 (2)	46 (3)	48 (3)	38 (4)	56 (2)	46 (3)	51 (2)	46 (2)	55 (2)
Challenge	29 (4)	28 (4)	32 (4)	25 (4)	30 (5)	22 (7)	24 (5)	21 (7)	27 (5)	25 (5)	26 (5)	23 (5)
Salary	26 (5)	34 (3)	43 (3)	26 (3)	45 (4)	54 (2)	63 (1)	45 (4)	35 (4)	40 (3)	45 (3)	35 (4)
Recognition	10 (6)	14 (7)	13 (6)	15 (7)	18 (7)	24 (6)	23 (6)	25 (6)	15 (6)	24 (6)	25 (6)	22 (7)
Prestige	9 (7)	15 (6)	13 (6)	16 (6)	19 (6)	25 (5)	22 (7)	28 (5)	13 (7)	24 (6)	25 (6)	23 (5)

NOTE: Pairs of shaded cells indicate responses where differences exceeded the sampling tolerance and are therefore significant. Gray = adults vs. all teens. Black = boys vs. girls.

Adults in the initial sample classified as "not informed" were more than twice as likely as informed adults to believe salary was extremely important to career choice (35 vs. 16%). Among Hispanics, informed adults were significantly more likely than those in the not informed group to believe interesting work and challenging work were extremely important.

Teens universally rated interesting work as the most important factor in choosing a career. Making a difference was second most important among teens in the initial and Hispanic samples and as important to job availability for African American teens. When gender was taken into account, African American girls were significantly more likely than African American boys to look for a job that makes a difference. Salary was a strong second choice for African American teens and the top choice among African American boys, who were significantly more likely than African American girls to consider salary extremely important.

Familiarity with the Profession

Survey participants were asked to rate, on a scale of 1 to 10, how well they understood what people in the six professions do on a day-to-day basis (Table 3-4). Adults and teens were both most familiar with what teachers and doctors do for a living. This is not surprising considering how doctors and teachers are portrayed in the media and that people naturally come into contact with them. Engineer, architect, and scientist were much less understood, and among teens, engineer was either the least understood or was tied with scientist for that distinction. Boys in all three samples claimed greater familiarity with engineering than girls.

Informed adults in the initial and Hispanic samples claimed a statistically greater familiarity with engineering than their not informed peers. Men in all three samples asserted greater knowledge of engineering than the women.

TABLE 3-4 Familiarity with Professionals, from 1 ("Don't Know at All") to 10 ("Know Very Well"), Adults, Teens, and Teens by Gender, Mean Score (Rank)

	Initial Sample				African American Oversample				Hispanic Oversample			
	Adults	Teens			Adults	Teens			Adults	Teens		
Professional		All	Boys	Girls		All	Boys	Girls		All	Boys	Girls
Teacher	8.18 (1)	8.85 (1)	8.84 (1)	8.85 (1)	8.8 (1)	8.4 (1)	8.1 (1)	8.7 (1)	8.3 (1)	8.6 (1)	8.5 (1)	8.8 (1)
Doctor	7.35 (2)	7.28 (2)	7.3 (2)	7.26 (2)	8 (2)	7.6 (2)	7.2 (2)	8 (2)	7.6 (2)	7.2 (2)	6.9 (2)	7.5 (2)
Lawyer	6.65 (3)	6.33 (3)	6.61 (3)	6.09 (3)	7.5 (3)	6.7 (3)	6.5 (2)	6.9 (3)	6.9 (3)	6.3 (3)	6.1 (3)	6.4 (3)
Engineer	5.75 (4)	4.86 (6)	5.41 (5)	4.4 (6)	5.8 (6)	5.2 (5)	5.7 (5)	4.7 (6)	5.8 (5)	5.2 (5)	5.7 (5)	4.8 (6)
Architect	5.66 (5)	4.99 (5)	5.2 (6)	4.81 (5)	5.9 (4)	5.5 (4)	5.8 (4)	5.2 (4)	6 (4)	5.7 (4)	6 (4)	5.5 (4)
Scientist	5.34 (6)	5.46 (4)	5.68 (4)	5.27 (4)	5.9 (4)	5.2 (5)	5.3 (6)	5.1 (5)	5.6 (6)	5.2 (5)	5.1 (6)	5.3 (5)

Attributes of Engineers

In answer to the only open-ended question, respondents were asked to type the first word or words that came to mind when they heard the word engineering. The words mentioned most often (22 to 30% of the time) by adults were "builders," "building," and "construction" (Table 3-5). The second most frequent associations for adults in the initial sample were "math" or "science" (mentioned by 12%) and "design" (mentioned by 11%). Among African American and Hispanic adults, "math" and "science" were the second most frequent words associated with engineering. Teens across the board typed "math" or "science" most often (between 21 and 31% of the time). Informed adults in all three samples were significantly more likely than the not informed cohorts to associate math and science with engineering.

The prominence of math and science in the minds of the public was reinforced by responses to a second question in which respondents were asked to decide how well each of 25 attributes described engineering and/or engineers. Adults and teens chose "high skill level in mathematics and science" as the most distinguishing attribute of engineering (Table 3-6). Only in the Hispanic oversample was there a difference between the informed and not informed subpopulations in views about mathematics and science, with the former believing more strongly in the essentiality of such skills. A majority of adults and teens also chose "designers," "builders," and "problem solvers." More teens than adults chose "hard workers." African American women were more likely than African American men to believe engineers are well paid, hard working, and smart.

Although in the in-depth interviews, engineers said they believed the public viewed them as "boring" and "nerdy," fewer than 15 percent of adults or teens in the survey described engineers this way, although teens in the initial sample were three times as likely as adults in that group to consider engineering "boring" and twice as likely to consider engineers "nerdy."

Hispanic girls were significantly more likely than Hispanic boys to think engineers were nerdy and boring. When answer choices "very well" and "somewhat well" were combined, Hispanic girls were also significantly less likely than Hispanic boys to consider engineering fun.

Hispanic girls were also significantly less likely than Hispanic boys to believe engineering has a positive effect on people's lives. These findings suggest Hispanic girls may be an important audience segment to reach with messaging.

Examples of Engineering

Survey respondents were asked to rate the relative appeal of 27 technologies (Table 3-7). In general, technologies that have not yet been developed or are not in widespread commercial use were more appealing to adults and teens than technologies already in use. The development of machines to enable blind people to see, cars that can run on alternate fuels, safer cars, and improved medical imaging devices were considered "very appealing" by most adults and teens. Teens across the board found entertainment technologies, such as iPods and video games, more appealing than adults did.

Fabric technologies, Velcro®, and the development of new foods were relatively unappealing to both adults and teens. Although Hispanic boys found fabric technologies and Velcro® significantly more appealing than Hispanic girls did, these technologies were still at the bottom of the boys' list.

Among all teens, computer processors, video games, and high-definition television were significantly more appealing to boys than to girls. And girls in the initial sample and the African American oversample found the idea of using DNA evidence to solve crimes much more appealing than boys did. Boys in the initial sample were much more strongly attracted to space exploration than girls, and boys in the initial sample and Hispanic oversample found missile-defense systems more appealing than did girls in these groups.

Message Testing

After refinement based on the results of qualitative research, the committee tested five messages in the online survey (Box 3-2). Like the preliminary message themes, the refined messages are all derived from the positioning statement.

TABLE 3-5 Words Most Often Associated with "Engineering" or "Engineer" (chosen by 5 percent or more of respondents), Percentage (rank)

Words Associated with Engineering	Initial Sample				African American Oversample				Hispanic Oversample			
	Adults	Teens			Adults	Teens			Adults	Teens		
		All	Boys	Girls		All	Boys	Girls		All	Boys	Girls
Builders/ buildings/ constuction/ bridges	23 (1)	16 (2)	17 (1)	15 (2)	29 (1)	21 (3)	23 (3)	19 (3)	30 (1)	25 (2)	25 (2)	26 (2)
Math/numbers/ physics/ computers/ science	12 (2)	21 (1)	17 (1)	23 (1)	17 (2)	27 (1)	24 (2)	30 (1)	19 (2)	31 (1)	35 (1)	28 (1)
Design	12 (2)	6 (5)	10 (4)	3 (6)	8 (4)	2 (10)	2 (10)	3 (9)	11 (3)	4 (11)	6 (9)	2 (11)
Mechanic/ machines/ industrial	5 (4)	13 (3)	13 (3)	14 (3)	10 (3)	23 (2)	26 (1)	20 (2)	10 (4)	21 (3)	21 (3)	21 (3)
Smart/skilled	5 (4)	1 (12)	2 (8)	1 (12)	5 (7)	2 (10)	1 (11)	3 (9)	7 (5)	3 (12)	3 (10)	2 (11)

Invention/ innovation/ creativity	5 (4)	3 (6)	2 (8)	4 (5)	5 (7)	3 (5)	3 (8)	2 (12)	6 (6)	6 (6)	7 (6)	6 (6)
Problem solving	3 (7)	3 (6)	5 (5)	* (12)	7 (5)	6 (6)	3 (8)	8 (5)	4 (9)	5 (8)	3 (10)	7 (5)
Electrical/ electronics	3 (7)	3 (6)	3 (7)	2 (7)	6 (6)	6 (6)	7 (6)	5 (7)	6 (6)	7 (5)	10 (5)	5 (8)
Complicated/ complex/difficult	2 (7)	2 (8)	2 (8)	2 (7)	3 (10)	2 (12)	* (12)	3 (8)	3 (10)	5 (8)	4 (12)	6 (6)
Cars/ Automotive/ trains	2 (10)	7 (4)	4 (6)	10 (4)	5 (7)	16 (4)	17 (4)	15 (4)	5 (8)	14 (4)	14 (4)	15 (4)
Technology	2 (10)	2 (8)	2 (8)	2 (8)	1 (12)	8 (5)	9 (5)	7 (6)	3 (10)	6 (6)	7 (6)	5 (8)
Makes things/ manufacturing	2 (10)	2 (8)	2 (8)	2 (8)	3 (10)	4 (8)	4 (7)	4 (8)	3 (10)	5 (8)	7 (6)	3 (10)

* less than 1%.

NOTE: Pairs of shaded cells indicate responses where differences exceeded the sampling tolerance and are therefore significant. Gray = adults vs. all teens. Black = boys vs. girls.

TABLE 3-6 Words That Describe Engineering "Very Well," by Percentage (rank)

Words that Describe Engineering	Initial Sample				African American Oversample				Hispanic Oversample			
	Adults	Teens			Adults	Teens			Adults	Teens		
		All	Boys	Girls		All	Boys	Girls		All	Boys	Girls
Good at math/science	86 (1)	84 (1)	85 (1)	84 (1)	77 (1)	71 (1)	59 (4)	81 (1)	72 (1)	76 (1)	74 (1)	78 (1)
Designs, draws, and plans things	61 (2)	63 (2)	64 (3)	61 (3)	67 (2)	59 (3)	60 (2)	59 (3)	60 (3)	56 (4)	61 (3)	50 (7)
Problem solver	59 (3)	62 (3)	68 (2)	57 (5)	60 (6)	52 (5)	58 (5)	47 (9)	64 (2)	50 (7)	47 (9)	53 (4)
Builds, constructs, and makes things	53 (4)	59 (5)	59 (4)	59 (4)	63 (3)	59 (3)	60 (2)	59 (3)	54 (4)	61 (2)		58 (2)
Creative	45 (5)	47 (7)	55 (7)	41 (9)	62 (4)	50 (6)	50 (6)	50 (7)	47 (6)	52 (5)	52 (6)	53 (4)
Get results	44 (6)	41 (10)	44 (9)	40 (10)	51 (8)	45 (8)	39 (8)	50 (7)	45 (8)	47 (8)	56 (5)	38 (11)
Well paid	44 (6)	46 (8)	48 (8)	44 (8)	61 (5)	45 (8)	32 (14)	56 (5)	53 (5)	51 (6)	52 (6)	51 (6)
Must be smart	43 (8)	56 (6)	58 (5)	54 (6)	46 (9)	37 (12)	35 (13)	38 (12)	45 (8)	42 (9)	38 (15)	45 (8)
Original thinkers	43 (8)	45 (9)	44 (9)	45 (7)	41 (12)	46 (7)	36 (9)	54 (6)	38 (13)	37 (12)	39 (13)	35 (12)
Hard working	42 (10)	62 (3)	56 (6)	66 (2)	56 (7)	64 (2)	63 (1)	65 (2)	47 (6)	58 (3)	58 (4)	58 (2)
Well respected	39 (11)	34 (14)	35 (15)	32 (13)	40 (14)	35 (14)	36 (9)	34 (16)	42 (10)	36 (14)	40 (11)	31 (13)
Work is rewarding	36 (12)	32 (15)	39 (13)	26 (15)	41 (12)	31 (17)	32 (14)	30 (17)	38 (13)	35 (15)	39 (13)	30 (14)

Mostly men	35 (13)	37 (12)	37 (14)	38 (12)	40 (14)	41 (11)	36 (9)	45 (10)	31 (15)	30 (16)	31 (17)	28 (15)
Have a positive effect	32 (14)	36 (13)	43 (12)	29 (14)	44 (11)	36 (13)	36 (9)	36 (14)	39 (12)	37 (12)	51 (8)	22 (17)
Inventors	28 (15)	41 (10)	44 (9)	39 (11)	46 (9)	43 (10)	45 (7)	40 (11)	40 (11)	42 (9)	40 (11)	43 (9)
Leaders	23 (16)	22 (16)	24 (16)	21 (16)	30 (17)	33 (16)	31 (16)	35 (15)	31 (15)	42 (9)	44 (10)	40 (10)
Often work outdoors	17 (17)	20 (17)	22 (17)	19 (17)	29 (18)	35 (14)	30 (17)	38 (12)	21 (18)	30 (16)	33 (16)	27 (16)
White	12 (18)	11 (23)	10 (22)	12 (22)	34 (16)	14 (21)	15 (20)	12 (21)	22 (17)	10 (23)	9 (22)	10 (24)
Entrepreneur	12 (18)	18 (18)	18 (18)	18 (18)	21 (19)	22 (19)	15 (20)	28 (18)	14 (21)	24 (18)	29 (18)	19 (19)
Too much school	10 (20)	15 (19)	15 (20)	15 (20)	16 (20)	14 (21)	17 (19)	11 (22)	18 (19)	13 (21)	12 (21)	15 (21)
Fun	7 (21)	9 (24)	6 (24)	11 (24)	15 (22)	15 (20)	12 (22)	17 (20)	13 (22)	19 (20)	24 (19)	14 (23)
Start new companies	7 (21)	14 (20)	16 (19)	12 (22)	16 (20)	23 (18)	23 (18)	24 (19)	18 (19)	21 (19)	20 (20)	22 (17)
Nerdy	5 (23)	14 (20)	13 (21)	15 (20)	13 (23)	10 (23)	10 (23)	10 (24)	12 (23)	12 (22)	4 (24)	18 (20)
Boring	4 (24)	12 (22)	7 (23)	16 (19)	6 (24)	10 (23)	10 (23)	11 (22)	9 (25)	10 (23)	4 (24)	15 (21)
Sits at a desk	2 (25)	6 (25)	5 (25)	7 (25)	4 (25)	3 (25)	1 (25)	5 (25)	12 (23)	5 (25)	7 (23)	4 (25)

NOTE: Pairs of shaded cells indicate responses where differences exceeded the sampling tolerance and are therefore significant. Gray = adults vs. all teens. Black = boys vs. girls.

TABLE 3-7 Examples of Engineering Considered "Very Appealing," by Percentage (rank)

Example	Initial Sample				African American Oversample				Hispanic Oversample			
	Adults	Teens			Adults	Teens			Adults	Teens		
		All	Boys	Girls		All	Boys	Girls		All	Boys	Girls
Machines that allow blind people to see	60 (1)	48 (2)	50 (3)	47 (3)	62 (1)	50 (1)	43 (9)	48 (2)	57 (2)	56 (2)	61 (2)	51 (2)
Building cars that run on alternative fuels	58 (2)	51 (1)	54 (2)	48 (2)	55 (3)	48 (2)	47 (6)	33 (13)	61 (1)	61 (1)	64 (1)	57 (1)
Protecting the water supply	54 (3)	37 (7)	36 (10)	39 (5)	46 (8)	29 (17)	23 (21)	22 (23)	50 (7)	46 (8)	48 (10)	44 (6)
Wind power	48 (4)	29 (18)	31 (21)	27 (16)	40 (12)	21 (23)	21 (22)	52 (1)	46 (11)	33 (17)	35 (19)	31 (14)
Creating more advanced MRI	47 (5)	32 (14)	29 (23)	35 (9)	54 (4)	48 (2)	43 (9)	31 (15)	54 (4)	48 (4)	49 (9)	48 (3)
Protecting rainforest by developing new ways to farm	47 (5)	40 (5)	35 (11)	45 (4)	40 (12)	26 (20)	19 (24)	35 (11)	49 (7)	42 (12)	44 (16)	40 (10)
Solar energy	47 (5)	35 (7)	35 (11)	35 (9)	47 (6)	36 (12)	37 (12)	46 (4)	56 (3)	45 (10)	52 (7)	38 (12)
Making cars safer	43 (8)	31 (15)	32 (20)	31 (13)	57 (2)	47 (5)	49 (5)	43 (5)	52 (5)	48 (4)	53 (6)	44 (6)
Using DNA to solve crimes	42 (9)	43 (4)	34 (15)	50 (1)	47 (6)	35 (13)	27 (14)	27 (18)	42 (12)	44 (11)	45 (15)	43 (8)

Space exploration	40 (10)	45 (3)	55 (1)	35 (9)	35 (20)	27 (18)	27 (14)	47 (3)	39 (14)	46 (8)	50 (8)	43 (8)
Making homes safer	40 (10)	27 (22)	24 (25)	29 (14)	52 (5)	44 (7)	40 (11)	42 (6)	49 (7)	38 (14)	41 (17)	36 (13)
Reducing air pollution	40 (10)	33 (13)	26 (24)	38 (6)	39 (14)	47 (5)	52 (4)	27 (18)	52 (5)	47 (6)	46 (12)	47 (5)
Smart traffic solutions	38 (13)	28 (20)	35 (11)	21 (19)	44 (10)	27 (18)	26 (16)	31 (15)	42 (12)	33 (17)	36 (18)	29 (16)
Missile defense systems	37 (14)	30 (17)	44 (5)	19 (23)	37 (17)	31 (14)	31 (13)	15 (23)	35 (16)	33 (17)	48 (10)	20 (25)
Turning deserts into farmland	37 (14)	25 (23)	33 (17)	17 (24)	39 (14)	15 (26)	15 (25)	36 (10)	34 (18)	29 (23)	32 (23)	26 (20)
DNA Test	34 (16)	34 (10)	33 (17)	36 (7)	31 (23)	31 (14)	24 (20)	39 (8)	35 (16)	29 (23)	34 (21)	24 (23)
Designing world's fastest plane	34 (16)	31 (15)	44 (5)	20 (22)	38 (16)	42 (9)	46 (7)	37 (9)	39 (14)	38 (14)	46 (12)	30 (15)
Making smaller, faster computer processor	34 (16)	34 (10)	44 (5)	26 (17)	44 (10)	48 (2)	60 (1)	35 (11)	49 (7)	47 (6)	56 (3)	39 (11)
Growing organs for transplant	32 (19)	35 (7)	37 (9)	33 (12)	32 (22)	30 (16)	25 (17)	26 (20)	32 (20)	31 (21)	32 (23)	29 (16)

continued

TABLE 3-7 Continued

Example	Initial Sample				African American Oversample				Hispanic Oversample			
	Adults	Teens			Adults	Teens			Adults	Teens		
		All	Boys	Girls		All	Boys	Girls		All	Boys	Girls
Building an acoustically perfect concert hall	27 (20)	29 (18)	34 (15)	24 (18)	37 (17)	26 (20)	25 (17)	25 (22)	27 (22)	31 (21)	34 (21)	28 (18)
Building the world's longest bridge	26 (21)	25 (23)	35 (11)	16 (25)	46 (8)	25 (22)	25 (17)	26 (20)	32 (20)	32 (20)	35 (19)	28 (18)
Developing new foods	24 (22)	25 (23)	31 (21)	21 (19)	23 (26)	19 (24)	11 (26)	32 (14)	23 (25)	21 (25)	23 (26)	19 (25)
HDTV	20 (23)	28 (20)	38 (8)	21 (19)	36 (19)	42 (9)	53 (3)	29 (17)	34 (18)	35 (16)	46 (12)	26 (20)
Designing video games	19 (24)	38 (6)	50 (3)	29 (14)	34 (21)	41 (11)	54 (2)	16 (25)	25 (24)	40 (13)	56 (3)	25 (22)
Developing new fabrics	13 (25)	13 (26)	9 (26)	16 (25)	25 (25)	18 (25)	21 (22)	41 (7)	23 (25)	16 (26)	25 (25)	9 (26)
iPod	13 (25)	34 (10)	33 (17)	36 (7)	27 (24)	43 (8)	44 (8)	9 (26)	27 (22)	51 (3)	55 (5)	48 (3)
Velcro	11 (27)	12 (27)	9 (26)	14 (27)	16 (27)	7 (27)	6 (27)	9 (26)	16 (27)	13 (27)	18 (27)	7 (27)

NOTE: Pairs of shaded cells indicate responses where differences exceeded the sampling tolerance and are therefore significant. Gray = adults vs. all teens. Black = boys vs. girls.

BOX 3-2
Messages Tested in the Online Survey

Engineers make a world of difference.*
From new farming equipment and safer drinking water to electric cars and faster microchips, engineers use their knowledge to improve people's lives in meaningful ways.

Engineers are creative problem-solvers.
They have a vision for how something should work and are dedicated to making it better, faster, or more efficient.

Engineers help shape the future.
They use the latest science, tools, and technology to bring ideas to life.

Engineering is essential to our health, happiness, and safety.
From the grandest skyscrapers to microscopic medical devices, it is impossible to imagine life without engineering.

Engineers connect science to the real world.
They collaborate with scientists and other specialists (such as animators, architects, or chemists) to turn bold new ideas into reality.

---

*This message was inspired by a similar theme used to promote National Engineers Week.

Three survey questions addressed responses to the messages. The first asked respondents how appealing the messages were and, separately, how believable and personally relevant they were (how much they cared about the message). Although the committee members were most concerned about the appeal of the messages, they recognized that an appealing message might not be believable, or vice versa. In some cases, a message might be believable but not considered relevant. In other cases, a very appealing message is likely to be considered personally relevant. By triangulating among appeal, believability, and relevance, the committee hoped to get an accurate sense of the validity of the appeal ratings.

All five tested messages were rated at least "somewhat appealing" by an overwhelming majority of adults and teens, a finding that reinforces the validity of the underlying positioning statement. The message with the highest "very appealing" rating—the most favorable category—among all adults and teens was "Engineers make a world of difference" (Figures 3-1 and 3-2). This message was also considered the

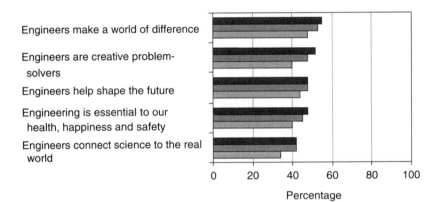

FIGURE 3-1 Messages selected as "very appealing" by adults, by percentage.
Note: Top bar = initial sample. Middle bar = African American oversample. Bottom bar = Hispanic oversample.

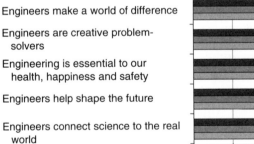

FIGURE 3-2 Messages selected as "very appealing" by teens, by percentage.
Note: Top bar = initial sample. Middle bar = African American oversample. Bottom bar = Hispanic oversample.

most believable and most relevant in most groups (Table 3-8). However, once again, girls were generally less enthusiastic than boys about all of the messages.

The message that received the lowest percentage of "very appealing" rankings by respondents in all groups was "Engineers connect science to the real world." This message was also the least personally

TABLE 3-8 Message Appeal, Believability, and Relevance Among Adults and Teens, by Percentages (rank)

	Initial Sample		African American Oversample		Hispanic Oversample	
Message	Adults	Teens	Adults	Teens	Adults	Teens
Engineers make a world of difference						
Very appealing	55 (1)	43 (1)	53 (1)	40 (1)	48 (1)	46 (1)
Very believable	57 (2)	54 (1)	57 (1)	40 (3)	49 (1)	47 (1)
Care very much	41 (1)	31 (1)	46 (1)	32 (2)	39 (1)	37 (1)
Engineers are creative problem-solvers						
Very appealing	52 (2)	42 (2)	48 (2)	33 (4)	40 (3)	39 (3)
Very believable	58 (1)	53 (2)	54 (2)	39 (4)	44 (4)	44 (3)
Care very much	32 (4)	26 (3)	38 (5)	27 (4)	33 (4)	30 (4)
Engineers help shape the future						
Very appealing	48 (3)	37 (3)	48 (2)	37 (2)	44 (2)	40 (2)
Very believable	56 (4)	48 (4)	53 (3)	46 (1)	45 (3)	46 (2)
Care very much	33 (3)	25 (4)	41 (2)	31 (3)	34 (3)	31 (2)
Engineering is essential to our health, happiness, and safety						
Very appealing	48 (3)	35 (4)	45 (4)	35 (3)	40 (3)	36 (4)
Very believable	57 (2)	50 (3)	49 (4)	35 (5)	47 (2)	39 (4)
Care very much	38 (2)	31 (1)	40 (3)	33 (1)	35 (2)	31 (2)
Engineering connects science to the real world						
Very appealing	42 (5)	35 (4)	42 (5)	31 (5)	34 (5)	35 (5)
Very believable	49 (5)	46 (5)	49 (4)	41 (2)	38 (5)	39 (4)
Care very much	28 (5)	21(5)	39 (4)	23 (5)	29 (5)	27 (5)

NOTE: Pairs of shaded cells indicate responses where differences between adults and teens exceeded the sampling tolerance and are therefore significant.

relevant to all but African American adults. The lack of resonance with this message was confirmed when survey participants were asked to choose the single "most appealing" message of the five (Figures 3-3 and 3-4).

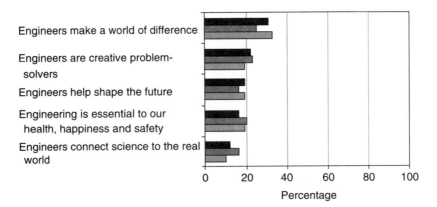

FIGURE 3-3 Messages selected as "most appealing" by adults, by percentage. Note: Top bar = initial sample. Middle bar = African American oversample. Bottom bar = Hispanic oversample.

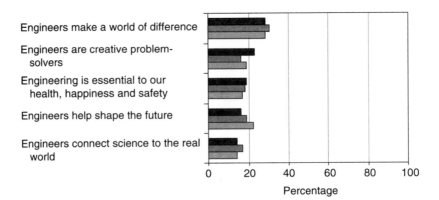

FIGURE 3-4 Messages selected as "most appealing" by teens, by percentage. Note: Top bar = initial sample. Middle bar = African American oversample. Bottom bar = Hispanic oversample.

Boys in the initial sample found "Engineering makes a world of difference" and "Engineers are creative problem solvers" equally appealing (Table 3-9). This second message did not appeal nearly as much to girls. The second most appealing message for girls, across the board, was "Engineering is essential to our health, happiness, and safety." Girls age 16 and 17 in the African American oversample and all girls in the Hispanic oversample found the "essential to health and happiness" message significantly more appealing than did the boys in those groups. Informed adults in the Hispanic and African American oversamples were significantly more positive than their not informed counterparts about all but one message: Engineers are creative problem-solvers.

As a check on both adult and teen preferences, respondents were also asked to choose a single "least appealing" message (Tables 3-10 and 3-11). "Engineers connect science to the real world" was the least

TABLE 3-9 "Most Appealing" Message, Teens by Gender and Percentage (rank)

Message	Initial Sample		African American Oversample		Hispanic Oversample	
	Boys	Girls	Boys	Girls	Boys	Girls
Engineers make a world of difference	27 (2)	30 (1)	28 (1)	32 (1)	30 (1)	26 (1)
Engineers help shape the future	16 (3)	16 (4)	20 (2)	18 (3)	26 (2)	19 (3)
Engineers are creative problem-solvers	28 (1)	19 (3)	18 (4)	14 (4)	20 (3)	18 (4)
Engineering is essential to our health, happiness and safety	16 (3)	22 (2)	14 (5)	22 (2)	12 (4)	21 (2)
Engineers connect science to the real world	13 (5)	13 (5)	20 (2)	14 (4)	12 (4)	16 (5)

NOTE: Pairs of shaded cells indicate responses where differences between boys and girls exceeded the sampling tolerance and are therefore significant.

TABLE 3-10 "Least Appealing" Message, Teens by Gender and Percentage (rank)

Message	Initial Sample		African American Oversample		Hispanic Oversample	
	Boys	Girls	Boys	Girls	Boys	Girls
Engineers make a world of difference	17 (3)	13 (5)	10 (5)	14 (5)	10 (5)	13 (5)
Engineers help shape the future	16 (5)	24 (2)	21 (2)	24 (1)	24 (2)	27 (1)
Engineers are creative problem-solvers	21 (2)	16 (4)	18 (4)	20 (3)	12 (4)	17 (4)
Engineers connect science to the real world	29 (1)	25 (1)	21 (2)	24 (1)	30 (1)	20 (3)
Engineering is essential to our health, happiness and safety	17 (3)	24 (2)	30 (1)	19 (4)	23 (3)	23 (2)

NOTE: Pairs of shaded cells indicate responses where differences between boys and girls exceeded the sampling tolerance and are therefore significant.

appealing message for all but African American boys, who found the message "Engineering is essential to our health, happiness, and safety" least appealing, and Hispanic girls, who found the message "Engineers help shape the future" least appealing. Among Hispanic adults, women reacted more positively to "Engineers are creative problem solvers" than men.

Preliminary Testing of Taglines

Several preliminary taglines (Box 3-3) were tested, although, because of time and funding constraints, the taglines were developed quickly without creative prototypes (such as posters, TV ads, or web pages) or input from focus groups. Thus the survey results do not represent the best measure of the potential (or lack of potential) of

TABLE 3-11 "Least Appealing" Message, Adults by Gender and Percentage (rank)

Message	Initial Sample		African American Oversample		Hispanic Oversample	
	Men	Women	Men	Women	Men	Women
Engineers make a world of difference	11 (5)	13 (5)	12 (5)	8 (5)	13 (5)	10 (5)
Engineers help shape the future	16 (4)	19 (2)	20 (3)	24 (3)	20 (3)	20 (3)
Engineers are creative problem-solvers	22 (3)	17 (3)	24 (2)	16 (4)	14 (4)	23 (2)
Engineers connect science to the real world	25 (1)	34 (1)	25 (1)	26 (1)	28 (1)	26 (1)
Engineering is essential to our health, happiness and safety	25 (1)	16 (4)	19 (4)	25 (2)	26 (2)	20 (3)

NOTE: Pairs of shaded cells indicate responses where differences between boys and girls exceeded the sampling tolerance and are therefore significant.

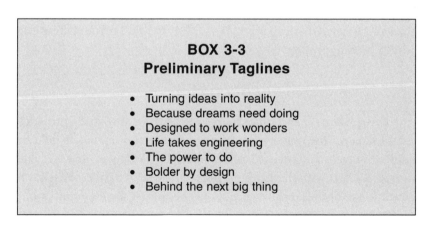

BOX 3-3
Preliminary Taglines

- Turning ideas into reality
- Because dreams need doing
- Designed to work wonders
- Life takes engineering
- The power to do
- Bolder by design
- Behind the next big thing

these taglines. Nevertheless, it was encouraging that several of them tested well.

"Turning ideas into reality" tested well among all survey respondents (Figures 3-5 and 3-6). This straightforward tagline, which is consistent with the messaging used by National Engineers Week, is more descriptive than evocative. It states plainly that engineers translate creative thinking into practical solutions. Perhaps that is one reason it scored well as a tagline. By itself, without any additional creative context, it makes the most sense.

It is interesting to note, however, that "Turning ideas into reality" was part of the key message, "Engineers connect science to the real world," which was the least appealing of the five tested messages, especially among women. This discrepancy reinforces the need for qualitative testing of taglines.

The second most appealing tagline varied among the sample populations. African American teens, for example, favored, "Designed to work wonders." The second favorite choice of adults and teens in the initial sample and the Hispanic oversample was "Because dreams need doing." The similar responses of girls and boys in all three populations to this tagline (Table 3-12) suggests that "Because dreams need doing" may be relatively gender neutral. Among Hispanic teens, there were significant gender differences for three of the seven taglines. Among African American teens, girls ages 16–17 were significantly more likely than all African American boys (44 vs. 29%) to find "Turning ideas into reality" very appealing.

CONCLUSION

The qualitative and quantitative research for this study provided useful data on the perceptions of engineering and engineers held by adults and teens and focused attention on the particular messages that resonated most with the sample groups. The research process itself was educational for the committee, not only because it shed light on public understanding of engineering, but also because it provided insights into the benefits and limitations of market research. Key findings from all of the research for this study are summarized in the annex to this chapter.

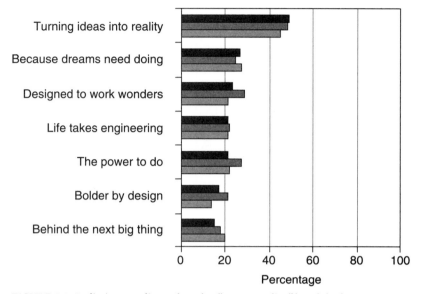

FIGURE 3-5 Preliminary taglines selected as "very appealing" by adults, by percentage. Note: Top bar = initial sample. Middle bar = African American oversample. Bottom bar = Hispanic oversample.

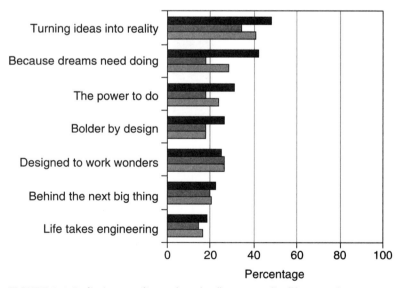

FIGURE 3-6 Preliminary taglines selected as "very appealing" by teens, by percentage. Note: Top bar = initial sample. Middle bar = African American oversample. Bottom bar = Hispanic oversample.

TABLE 3-12 Preliminary Taglines Selected as "Very Appealing" by Adults, Teens, and Teens by Gender, by Percentage (rank)

Tagline	Initial Sample				African American Oversample				Hispanic Oversample			
	Adults	Teens			Adults	Teens			Adults	Teens		
		All	Boys	Girls		All	Boys	Girls		All	Boys	Girls
Turning ideas into reality	46 (1)	48 (1)	54 (1)	43 (1)	48 (1)	34 (1)	29 (1)	38 (1)	45 (1)	41 (1)	47 (1)	35 (1)
Because dreams need doing	24 (2)	42 (2)	43 (2)	42 (2)	24 (4)	18 (4)	17 (6)	18 (4)	27 (2)	28 (2)	28 (3)	28 (2)
The power to do	20 (3)	31 (3)	37 (3)	25 (3)	27 (3)	18 (4)	21 (4)	16 (6)	22 (3)	24 (4)	28 (3)	20 (4)
Bolder by design	18 (6)	26 (4)	33 (4)	20 (6)	21 (6)	18 (4)	16 (7)	19 (3)	14 (7)	18 (6)	22 (6)	15 (5)
Designed to work wonders	20 (3)	25 (5)	29 (5)	21 (4)	28 (2)	26 (2)	26 (2)	25 (2)	21 (4)	26 (3)	32 (2)	21 (3)
Behind the next big thing	14 (7)	23 (6)	26 (6)	21 (4)	18 (7)	20 (3)	23 (3)	17 (5)	20 (6)	21 (5)	27 (5)	15 (5)
Life takes engineering	20 (3)	19 (7)	24 (7)	15 (7)	22 (5)	15 (7)	20 (5)	12 (7)	21 (4)	17 (7)	19 (7)	14 (7)

NOTE: Pairs of shaded cells indicate responses where differences exceeded the sampling tolerance and are therefore significant. Gray = adults vs. all teens. Black = boys vs. girls.

One of the most important outcomes of the research was to demonstrate how much perceptions of mathematics and science have shaped perceptions of engineering. Evidently, messages from the engineering community linking success in engineering to skills in mathematics and science have reached a wide audience. Although this message is correct, our research suggests that it has not been effective in improving the appeal of engineering.

The committee received more public comments on the linkage of science and mathematics to engineering than on any other subject. Several people suggested that attracting more students to engineering will ultimately require improving the teaching of math and science, including how applications of math and science are relevant to students.

Another result of our research was to demonstrate that age and gender affect perceptions of engineering and engineers. The differences were most evident in the online survey. For example, adults, who have much more experience in the world of work than teens, were generally more concerned about job availability. One implication of this difference for messaging is to keep in mind that adults, who may influence students' career choices, may be especially sensitive to reports (accurate or not) of the outsourcing of technical jobs, including engineering jobs, and the resultant possible decrease in employment opportunities.

The research strongly suggests that boys and girls have different reactions to messages and different perceptions of engineering. The focus groups and triads confirmed other research showing that girls are much more comfortable with images of engineering that include people, especially women, whereas boys tend to gravitate to "things." This suggests messaging that targets girls should include a human element.

Boys also appear to have a more positive outlook toward engineering as a career choice than girls, who are less confident that engineering can be a rewarding profession that will have a positive effect on people's lives. This relatively negative view of engineering has been documented in other research (EWEP, 2005; EWEP, unpublished). Girls also were generally less responsive to all of the messages tested in this project.

The research also exposed a "disconnect" between the engineering community's self-perception and the public perception of engineers. The image of a nerdy, dull person, as popularized in the comic strip *Dilbert*, is widely accepted as a given by the engineering community. However, our research shows Dilbert is not the public's image of an engineer. Neither adults nor teens in our study correlated Dilbert's characteristics with real engineers. This means that messaging resources that might have been invested in efforts to counter the "nerdiness" image can be spent in more productive ways.

Finally, the research shows there are few significant ethnicity-based differences in the way adults and teens perceive engineers, engineering, and messages and taglines meant to improve the image of engineering. This does not mean, however, that messaging efforts, particularly the use of taglines, should not take ethnicity, culture, language, and other factors into account. For optimum effectiveness, messaging needs to be contextualized for the target population.

REFERENCES

College Board. 2007. PSAT/NMSQT® 2006-2007 College-Bound High School Juniors Summary Report, Table 7: College Major. Available online at *http://www.collegeboard. com/prod_downloads/about/news_info/cbjunior/yr2006/AL.pdf.* (October 26, 2007)

Cunningham, C., C. Lachapelle, and A. Lindgren-Streicher. 2005. Assessing Elementary School Students Conceptions of Engineering and Technology. Proceedings of the 2005 American Society for Engineering Education Annual Conference and Exposition. Portland, Ore., June 12–15. Washington, D.C.: ASEE.

DeNavas-Walt, C., B.D. Proctor, and J. Smith. 2007. Income, Poverty, and Health Insurance Coverage in the United States: 2006. Table A-1, Households by total money income, race, and Hispanic origin of householder: 1967–2006. Current Population Reports—Consumer Income. U.S. Census Bureau. U.S. Department of Commerce. Issued August 2007. Available online at *http://www.census.gov/prod/2007pubs/p60-233.pdf.* (January 31, 2008)

EWEP (Extraordinary Women Engineers Project). 2005. Extraordinary Women Engineers—Final Report, April 2005. Available online at *http://www.eweek.org/site/news/ Eweek/EWE_Needs_Asses.pdf.* (July 16, 2007)

EWEP. Unpublished. January 2007 memorandum from Global Strategy Group to the Extraordinary Women Engineers Project.

Lippa, R. 1998. Gender-related individual differences and the structure of vocational interests: The importance of the people-things dimension. Journal of Personality and Social Psychology 74: 996–1009.

U.S. Census Bureau. 2006. Historical Income Tables—Households, Table H-13, Educational attainment of householder households with householder 25 years old and over by median and mean income: 1991–2005. Available online at *www.census. gov/hhes/www/income/histinc/h13.html.* (January 31, 2008)

ANNEX
SUMMARY OF KEY RESEARCH FINDINGS

This annex consolidates the most important research findings from this project. By putting all of the information in one place, the committee hopes to help readers identify results most relevant to their needs. Since no two outreach efforts are likely to use identical tactics or share the same purpose or target audience, certain findings will be more significant for some readers than for others. The committee organized the annex to reflect the very important idea of audience segmentation. Thus, findings that call out differences in attitudes or understanding between teens and adults are grouped together, as are findings for boys and girls, men and women, and informed and not informed adults. When used in concert with the detailed data presented in the body of Chapter 3, the annex should be a useful guide for designing effective outreach to improve public understanding of engineering.

FOCUS GROUPS AND TRIADS

Students

The majority of students understand that engineers "design and build things" but tend to have a very limited idea of what engineers actually do.

Students do not have an overtly negative impression of engineers, but many feel that they are not smart enough or do not enjoy math or science enough to become engineers themselves.

Many students think that engineers are sedentary, work mostly on computers, and have little contact with other people.

Most girls believe that women have the talent and intellect to become engineers, if they so choose.

When asked to name engineers they knew or had heard of, including those who had come to their schools on career days, most students could name only men.

Examples of engineering related to the objects and activities of students' daily lives aroused a great deal of interest.

"Making good money" was the career goal mentioned most often by students.[3] The idea of "helping make a difference" also had a very strong appeal.

Parents

Parents were mostly of the opinion that engineering would provide their child with job security in the form of good salary and benefits, as well as a career path that would enable them to continue to grow and succeed.

Parents tended to prefer the more practical messages, underscoring their concerns about job security for their children.

ONLINE SURVEY

General Findings

Both adults and teens said the most distinguishing characteristic of engineers is their high skill level in mathematics and science.

Less than 15 percent of adults or teens described engineers as "boring" or "nerdy."

Technologies that have yet to be developed or are not in widespread commercial use were more appealing to adults and teens than technologies already in use.

---

[3]This contrasted to the answers from teens in the online survey who rated the importance of salary to job choice second or third behind "interesting work" and "work that makes a difference, is meaningful."

"Engineers make a world of difference" was the message with the highest "very appealing" rating among all adult and teen groups.

"Engineers connect science to the real world" was the least appealing message among all survey groups and the least personally relevant for all but African American adults.

All teens rated interesting work as the most important consideration in choosing a career. Making a difference was second most important among teens in the initial sample and Hispanic teens, and equally important to job availability for African American teens.

Adults in the initial sample and Hispanic oversample rated interesting work and job availability as most important and of equal value in career choice. African American adults rated job availability most important and interesting work second.

Teens versus Adults

Teens in the initial sample were three times as likely as adults to consider engineering "boring" and twice as likely to consider engineers "nerdy."

More teens than adults considered engineers hard workers.

Teens across the board responded more strongly than adults to entertainment technologies, such as iPods and video games.

Informed versus "Not Informed" Adults

Adults in the initial sample classified as "not informed" were more than twice as likely as informed adults to believe salary was extremely important to career choice.

Informed adults in all three samples were significantly more likely than the not informed cohorts to associate math and science with engineering.

Informed adults in the Hispanic and African American oversamples were significantly more positive than their not informed counterparts about all but one message: Engineers are creative problem-solvers.

Men versus Women

African American women were more likely than African American men to believe engineers are well paid, hard working, and smart.

Men in all three samples asserted greater knowledge of engineering than did women.

Among Hispanic adults, women reacted more positively to "Engineers are creative problem solvers" than men.

Boys versus Girls

In all of the teen groups, boys were nearly twice as likely as girls to rate engineering as a very good career choice.

Boys in all three samples claimed they had greater familiarity with engineering than girls.

African American girls were significantly more likely than African American boys to want a job that "makes a difference."

African American boys were significantly more likely than African American girls to consider salary extremely important to job choice.

Hispanic girls were significantly more likely than Hispanic boys to think engineers were nerdy and boring.

Hispanic girls were significantly less likely than Hispanic boys to believe engineering has a positive effect on people's everyday lives.

In all teen groups, computer processors, video games, and high-definition television were significantly more appealing to boys than to girls.

Girls in the initial sample and African American oversample found the idea of using DNA evidence to solve crimes much more appealing than did boys in these populations.

Girls were generally less enthusiastic than boys about all of the messages.

Boys in the initial sample found "Engineering makes a world of difference" and "Engineers are creative problem solvers" equally appealing messages. The second message did not appeal nearly as much to girls.

After "Engineers make a world of difference," the second most appealing message for girls across the board was "Engineering is essential to our health, happiness and safety."

"Engineers connect science to the real world" was the least appealing message for all teens. However, African American boys disliked the "Engineering is essential to our health, happiness and safety" message most, and Hispanic girls disliked the "Engineers help shape the future" message most.

CONCLUSIONS
AND
RECOMMENDATIONS

The purpose of this project was to look beyond the engineering community and to change the longstanding pattern of self-initiated, ad hoc communications. To make this goal, the committee needed both an independent analysis of the situation and the advice of experienced, creative market-research professionals.

One unanticipated benefit of engaging outside professionals was that committee members were encouraged, indeed obliged, to become educated about the processes, benefits, and limitations of message development and testing. Another was that our many interactions with Bemporad Baranowski Marketing Group/Global Strategy Group led to a relationship of trust and mutual respect that facilitated our dialog about complex, sometimes difficult, issues.

Market research is as much an art as a science. Although it is desirable, and often feasible, to gather data via focus groups and surveys, gathering the right data, and doing it effectively, requires a professional approach based on judgment, experience, and common sense. Market research provided direction and a rationale for helping us allocate time, money, and human resources in developing our positioning statement and messages.

Happily, our research revealed that the public does not have a negative image of engineers. In fact, the public has a much more positive view of engineers than engineers seem to have of themselves. Most adults and teens in our samples respect engineers and believe that their work is both rewarding and important, although they also have a poor idea about what engineers do on a day-to-day basis. They also have a strong sense that engineering is not "for everyone," especially not for girls. The public understanding of engineering is strongly linked to just one aspect of the discipline—the need for mathematics and science skills. Other vital aspects of engineering, such as creativity, teamwork, and communication, are largely unknown.

Based on the results of our research, we can make a strong case that effective messaging will require different messages for different target audiences (see Table 3-10). For example, when branding engineers or marketing engineering to teens, we must take into account how their ideas of engineering and their interests differ from those of adults. In addition, messages for teens will have to be adapted to take into account gender, because girls and boys have different perspectives on engineering and different connections to it.

In the sections that follow, the committee presents conclusions and recommendations that will lead to strategic as well as tactical changes in the way the engineering community communicates with the public. In the first section, the committee addresses how the positioning statement, messages, and taglines should be used. The second section includes an argument for a centralized public relations "tool kit" for the engineering community. In the third section, the committee proposes an ambitious, long-term initiative—the development and implementation of a large-scale communications "campaign."

USING THE POSITIONING STATEMENT, MESSAGES, AND TAGLINES

We live in a society inundated with information and messages. More than 25 years ago, advertising experts Al Ries and Jack Trout lamented, "There's a traffic jam on the turnpikes of the mind" (Ries and Trout, 1981). Since then, the situation has gotten even worse. Publishers in the United States put out hundreds of thousands of books every year, viewers can choose from hundreds of television channels, and Internet users can instantaneously search billions of web pages via a variety of search engines.

To help break through the communications clutter, the committee recognized that it would be necessary to use modern mass-marketing techniques, which are commonly used in the commercial and political sectors but rarely used by the engineering community for public outreach. Up to now, efforts to promote a positive image of engineering have largely been based on opinions and educated guesses about the kinds of messages that will work. Decisions have been made by leadership and staff of engineering organizations that rarely reflect the makeup of the target populations of these messages (i.e., young people, girls, and underrepresented minorities). Although some individuals may have training in public relations or marketing, as far as the committee could tell, few engineering organizations have relied on the services of professional creative or market-research firms.

One of the most important findings of this study is the strong association in the minds of the public between engineering and competency in mathematics and science. "Must be good at math and science" was by far the most frequently selected attribute of engineers in our online surveys, indicating that messages emphasizing ability in mathematics and science as a prerequisite to the study of engineering have been absorbed by both adults and teenagers. Our testing also showed that the least appealing of five tested messages was the one that portrayed engineers as "connecting science to the real world."

From this, we concluded that, if we continue to overly emphasize math and science in marketing or rebranding engineering, we are likely to alienate or scare off youngsters, rather than attract them to engineering. We believe the same can be said about messages that focus on the practical benefits of being an engineer rather than the inspirational, optimistic aspects of engineering.

Recommendation 1. To present an effective case for the importance of engineering and the value of an engineering education, the engineering community should engage in coordinated, consistent, effective communication to "reposition" engineering. Specifically, the engineering community should adopt and actively promote the positioning statement (Box 4-1) in this report, which emphasizes that engineering and engineers can make a difference in the world, rather than describing engineering in terms of required skills and personal benefits. The statement should not appear verbatim in external communications but should be used as a point of reference, or anchor, for all public outreach.

Of course, mathematics and science will continue to be necessary skills for engineers. Math and science skills can last a lifetime and can also provide a springboard for careers in many fields. At this point, an analogy with the medical profession might be instructive for showing how a change in messaging might work. The medical profession, which depends heavily on science skills, does not market itself to young people by emphasizing that they will have to learn organic chemistry. Physicians are promoted as people who cure disease and relieve human suffering.

In marketing engineering, we too ought to appeal to the hopes and dreams of prospective students and the public. This approach will not only appeal to the higher aspirations of young people, but will also place math and science skills, correctly, as *one* of a variety of skills and

---

BOX 4-1
A Positioning Statement for Engineering

No profession unleashes the spirit of innovation like engineering. From research to real-world applications, engineers constantly discover how to improve our lives by creating bold new solutions that connect science to life in unexpected, forward-thinking ways. Few professions turn so many ideas into so many realities. Few have such a direct and positive effect on people's everyday lives. We are counting on engineers and their imaginations to help us meet the needs of the 21st century.

dispositions necessary for successful engineers, including collaboration, communication, and teamwork.

In addition to developing a new, powerful positioning statement, we created and tested several messages. Our research does not, and should not, preclude others from pursuing additional message development, but the committee believes that the rigorous process we used to generate our messages justifies their widespread use. In February 2008, the National Academy of Engineering launched a new website, Engineer Your Life (*www.engineeryourlife.org*), which aims to interest academically prepared high school girls in careers in engineering. The site used our message "Engineers make a world of difference" on its homepage and adopted other key words vetted in our research, such as creativity and problem-solving.

Recommendation 2. The four messages that tested well in this project—"Engineers make a world of difference," "Engineers are creative problem-solvers," "Engineers help shape the future," and "Engineering is essential to our health, happiness, and safety"—should be adopted by the engineering community in ongoing and new public outreach initiatives. The choice of a specific message should be based on the demographics of the target audience(s) and informed by the qualitative and quantitative data collected during this project.

Finally, the committee notes that, because of money and time constraints, we were not able to carry out a full creative process in the development of taglines, which would have led to many more possible taglines, presentations of the taglines in context, and testing of the contextualized taglines in focus groups. Nevertheless, the positive responses via online testing to several of the taglines suggest that they may be able to be effectively used for engineering-outreach projects. The committee believes the taglines should be further tested to identify and validate which ones might be appropriate for a broad-scale national campaign.

Recommendation 3. More rigorous research should go forward to identify and test a small number of taglines for a nationwide engineering-awareness campaign. The taglines should be consistent with the positioning statement and messages developed through this project and should take into account differences among target populations. In the interest of encouraging coordination among outreach activities, the results of this research should be made widely available to the engineering community.

CREATING A SHARED PUBLIC-RELATIONS RESOURCE

Engineering societies, universities, technology-based firms, federal laboratories, museums, and other organizations currently spend more than $400 million annually to promote public awareness of engineering (Davis and Gibbin, 2002). These ad hoc efforts, although praiseworthy in their intentions, have not succeeded, largely because their messages are not consistent. In addition, because of the discontinuous nature of these efforts, it has been impossible to develop effective metrics to measure their effectiveness and refine the messages accordingly. The committee concludes that, in the short term, consistent messages, even by a modest number of these organizations, could be a huge step forward in promoting a positive, appealing image of engineering.

Recommendation 4. To facilitate deployment of effective messages, an online public relations "tool kit" should be developed for the engineering community that includes information about research-based message-development initiatives and examples of how messages have and can be used effectively (e.g., in advertising, press releases, informational brochures, and materials for establishing institutional identity). The online site should also provide a forum for the sharing of information among organizations.

LAUNCHING A CAMPAIGN

Although making current messages more consistent is an important short-term goal, the committee concludes that a more explicit, coordinated approach is likely to yield better results in the long term. Thoughtful targeting of the messages and further refinement of the taglines for public outreach about engineering will be necessary, but not sufficient. Outreach efforts must be embedded in a larger strategic framework—a communications campaign driven by a strong brand positioning statement and involving a variety of communication methods. A campaign must include diverse messengers and be supported by dedicated resources. Finally, the campaign must include metrics for determining the effectiveness of its components and, equally important, must be given enough time to succeed.

In short, a campaign must reach multiple audiences in creative ways, using the following tools and techniques:

- traditional and online advertising;
- corporate partnerships/sponsorships;
- pop-culture initiatives (e.g., contests, games, books, TV specials, documentary projects);
- educational initiatives (e.g., curricula);
- outreach to young people, parents, educators, guidance counselors, and the media; and
- media training for ambassadors or spokespersons.

A campaign of the size and duration that will have a measurable impact on the public understanding of engineering will require significant resources. Our consultants proposed a "conservative" price tag of $12 million to $25 million per year for two or three years. This may be enough to launch a campaign, but the long-term costs could easily be higher. The recent "Got Milk?" campaign targeting teenagers cost $20 million annually (Levere, 2006), and the Centers for Disease Control and Prevention anti-obesity campaign, "Verb: It's What You Do," targeting young people ages 9 to 13, had a budget of $59 million in 2005 (Beirne, 2006).

Resources of this magnitude are not likely to be forthcoming from government or foundations. Thus the question arises as to whether the engineering community, particularly large and influential technology-focused corporations, will be willing to support such an initiative.

A second concern is how the campaign would be organized and carried out. Some degree of centralized planning will be necessary to ensure coordination and communication, which will require agreement by the major participants. There is already one cooperative out-reach venture in engineering, National Engineers Week, which might be leveraged for this purpose. We might, however, need a new structure to coordinate a campaign.

A final concern relates to the need for metrics to determine the effectiveness of messages and projects. Although measuring the outcomes of public outreach efforts is notoriously difficult, a campaign of this scope must include a substantial evaluation component to ensure that we can determine what works and improve upon elements that are not as effective as anticipated.

Recommendation 5. A representative cross section of the engineering community should convene to consider funding, logistics, and other aspects of a coordinated, multiyear communications campaign to improve the public understanding of engineering.

A FINAL WORD

The project described in this report was conducted according to a carefully designed process for developing messages to improve the public understanding of engineering. The approach included the services of professionals in the fields of communications and market research and required both quantitative and qualitative research methods. To ensure balance and accuracy, the report and the findings and recommendations were carefully vetted by outside experts, whose comments and suggestions led to improvements in the final document. The rigor of the study process should reassure the engineering community—and others interested in this important topic—that a tested set of tools is now available to promote a more positive image of engineering and engineers.

As suggested in Recommendation 4, we know that more work will be necessary to enrich, expand, and disseminate messaging resources, and, as noted in Recommendation 3, more research on taglines will be necessary. Neither of these requirements, however, should delay or discourage action by the engineering community. Even if the national campaign described in Recommendation 5 is not immediately forthcoming, creative implementation of messages and taglines can have an immediate impact. Combined efforts by multiple organizations following the same "playbook" can create positive momentum toward increasing the appeal of engineering to students, educators, parents, policy makers, and society at large.

The most significant outcome of this project is the recasting of engineering as articulated in the positioning statement. If this statement were adopted by the engineering community, as urged in Recommendation 1, we can not only reshape the self-images of engineers, but also empower engineers to communicate more confidently with the public. In this way, we may truly change the conversation.

REFERENCES

Beirne, M. 2005. CDC tries to take a bite out of childhood obesity. Ad Week. October 24, 2005.

Davis, L., and R. Gibbin. 2002. Raising Public Awareness of Engineering. Washington, D.C.: The National Academies Press.

Levere, J.L. 2006. Body by milk: More than just a white mustache. *New York Times*, Section C, p. 3, August 30, 2006.

Ries, A., and J. Trout. 1981. Positioning: The Battle for Your Mind. New York: Warner Books.

A   BIOGRAPHIES OF COMMITTEE MEMBERS

DON P. GIDDENS (NAE), *chair*, is dean of the College of Engineering (since 1992), Lawrence L. Gellerstedt Jr. Chair in Bioengineering, and Georgia Research Alliance Eminent Scholar, Georgia Institute of Technology. After receiving all three of his degrees (B.S.E. 1963, M.S. 1965, and Ph.D. 1966) from Georgia Tech, he joined the faculty there in 1968. Dean Giddens is a member of the National Academy of Engineering, the Biomedical Engineering Society, and the Big 10+ Deans Council, a founding fellow and past president of the American Institute for Medical and Biological Engineering, and fellow of the American Heart Association and American Society of Mechanical Engineers (ASME). He received the H.R. Lissner Award from ASME in 1993 and was the ASME Thurston Lecturer in 1996. In June 2007, he was elected chair of the Executive Board of the Engineering Deans Council of the American Society for Engineering Education. Dr. Giddens is a member of several advisory boards and councils for academic institutions, corporations, and professional societies. He is also the author of more than 300 refereed publications, book chapters, and presentations and maintains an active research program in cardiovascular hemodynamics at Georgia Tech.

RICK E. BORCHELT is director of communications at the Genetics and Public Policy Center, Berman Bioethics Center, Johns Hopkins University, where he also teaches science policy and politics in the science writing program. Previously, he was director of communications and public affairs at Whitehead Institute for Biomedical Research at Massachusetts Institute of Technology, an independent research enterprise. Mr. Borchelt's varied career includes stints as director of media relations for the National Academy of Sciences; press secretary for the U.S. House of Representatives Committee on Science, Space, and Technology; special assistant for public affairs in the Executive Office of the President during the Clinton Administration; and director of communications for the U.S. Department of Energy (DOE) Office of Science. He chaired a three-year study by a blue-ribbon panel of Pulitzer Prize–winning journalists, scientists, public affairs officers, and science writers, funded by DOE and the National Aeronautics and Space Administration, on best practices in communicating to the public about science, technology, and health, which culminated in an international conference in March 2002, "Communicating the Future." Mr. Borchelt is currently an advisor to a project funded by the National Science Foundation (NSF) on nanoscale informal science education. He was elected a fellow of the American Association for the Advancement of Science in 2004 and is a commentary editor for *Science Communication.*

VIRGIL R. CARTER is executive director of the American Society of Mechanical Engineers (ASME), where his responsibilities include overseeing budgets, staff, and technical and educational activities, as well as management of the ASME Foundation and affiliated business entities. His professional career spans 42 years and includes military service, executive and ownership positions in business, academic teaching and administration, and association management. After earning a Bachelor of Architecture degree from Oklahoma State University (OSU) in 1964, he served as a captain on a Special Forces A-Team in Vietnam. After the war, he earned a master's degree in architecture from the University of Illinois in 1969. In 1986, after 17 years of private architectural practice, he returned to OSU as head of the School of Architecture. From 1990 to 1996, Mr. Carter was senior executive at the American Institute of Architects, Washington, D.C., and in 1996 he founded Business & Educational Advisory Services, in Falls Church, Virginia. In 1997, be became executive director of the Project Management Institute, which experienced a 350 percent net growth in membership and expanded its global membership to 120 countries under his leadership. In 2002, he accepted his current position at ASME. Mr. Carter travels frequently throughout the world in support of ASME, engineering, and technology. He is a fellow of the American Institute of Architects and a member of several other organizations, including the American Society of Association Executives, the Pennsylvania Art Association, and the Special Forces Association.

WILLIAM S. HAMMACK, a professor of chemical and biomolecular engineering at the University of Illinois, Urbana-Champaign, earned a B.S. in chemical engineering from Michigan Technological University and an M.S. and Ph.D. from the University of Illinois. He taught for 10 years at Carnegie Mellon University before returning to Illinois, where he worked on outreach to the public to explain engineering and technology. He has created more than 300 pieces for pubic radio, which have been heard on "Marketplace" and around the world on Radio National Australia, for which he received the American Institute of Chemical Engineers Service to Society Award, the American Society of Mechanical Engineer's Edwin F. Church Medal, the American Society of Engineering Education's President's Award, the IEEE Award for Distinguished Literacy Contributions, the American Chemical Society's Grady-Stack Award, and the American Institute of Physics Science Writing Award. In addition, he teaches a General Education course on engineering for non-majors. He spent 2005–2006 on leave from the university as a Jefferson Science Fellow at the U.S. Department of State.

LEAH H. JAMIESON (NAE) is John A. Edwardson Dean of Engineering and Ransburg Distinguished Professor of Electrical and Computer Engineering, Purdue University; she also has a courtesy appointment in Purdue's Department of Engineering Education. Dr. Jamieson has been recognized for her achievements as co-founder (with Edward J. Coyle) and co-director (with William C. Oakes) of the Engineering Projects in Community Service (EPICS) Program, which was awarded the National Academy of Engineering's 2005 Bernard M. Gordon Prize for Innovation in Engineering and Technology Education. Also for EPICS-related activities, she (and Coyle) received the 1997 Chester F. Carlson Award for Innovation in Engineering Education from the American Society for Engineering Education, and Dean Jamieson received the IEEE Education Society 2000 Harriet B. Rigas "Outstanding Woman Engineering Educator" Award. Dr. Jamieson was one of the inaugural recipients of the NSF Director's Award for Distinguished Teaching Scholars (2001), was inducted into Purdue's Book of Great Teachers (2003), and was named 2002 Indiana Professor of the Year by the Carnegie Foundation and the Council for the Advancement and Support of Education. Dr. Jamieson has conducted research on speech analysis and recognition and the design of parallel processing algorithms and software for digital speech, image, and signal processing, and is the author of more than 175 papers and co-editor of *Algorithmically Specialized Parallel Computers* (Academic Press, 1985) and *The Characteristics of Parallel Algorithms* (MIT Press, 1987). She is 2007 president and CEO of IEEE and has held many other leadership positions at IEEE since 1998. She has also been associate editor and a member of the editorial board for several IEEE publications, a member of the Advisory Committee for the NSF Directorate for Computer and Information Science and Engineering (1998–2000), and a member (1998–2001, 2001–2004, 2005–2007) and secretary (1999–2001) of the Board of Directors of the Computing Research Association. She received her S.B. in mathematics from MIT and Ph.D. from Princeton University.

JAMES H. JOHNSON, JR., is a professor of civil engineering and dean of the College of Engineering, Architecture, and Computer Sciences at Howard University. He received his B.S. from Howard University, his M.S. from the University of Illinois, and his Ph.D. from the University of Delaware. His research interests include the treatment and disposal of hazardous substances, environmental policy in relation to minorities, nanomaterials in environmental restoration, and environmental curricula and strategies for increasing the participation of underrepresented groups in science, technology, engineering, and mathematics disciplines. A member of the National Research Council (NRC) Division of Earth and Life Sciences Oversight Committee, Environmental Protection Agency Science Advisory Board, American Society of Civil Engineers (ASCE) Committee on Diversity and Women in Civil Engineering, and vice chair of the Anne Arundel Community College (Maryland) Board of Trustees, he has also served on several university, private-sector, and research-center advisory committees, NRC boards and committees, and government advisory committees. The author of more than 60 scholarly articles, a contributor to three books, and co-editor of two books, Dr. Johnson is a registered professional engineer in the District of Columbia, a diplomate of the American Academy of Environmental Engineers, and the 2005 recipient of the National Society of Black Engineers Lifetime Achievement Award in Academia.

VIRGINIA KRAMER, executive creative director at the advertising and public relations firm Keiler & Co., oversees creative products of all kinds, including print and broadcast advertising, collateral products, direct mail products, and interactive products. Ms. Kramer is an award-winning copywriter with broad experience working with clients in a variety of industries, including financial services, banking, insurance, health care, aerospace, high technology, medical devices, pharmaceuticals, manufacturing, publishing, and the performing arts. Ms. Kramer graduated (magna cum laude) from the University of Hartford. She was a participant in the NAE preliminary focus group in April 2005 on public understanding of engineering messaging.

PATRICK J. NATALE is executive director of the American Society of Civil Engineers (ASCE) and the recipient of the 2006 Kenneth Andrew Roe Award from the American Association of Engineering Societies. Prior to joining ASCE in 2002, Mr. Natale was executive director of the National Society of Professional Engineers (NSPE), where he had been active in leadership and internal management for many years at both national and state levels. In 1997, Mr. Natale received the NSPE

Distinguished Service Award, and in July 2000, he was named a Fellow of the society. He was also president, national director, and practice division officer of the New Jersey Society of Professional Engineers. Mr. Natale had a 28-year career at Public Service Electric and Gas Company of New Jersey, where he held many top-level jobs. Over the years, he was responsible for managing sales, marketing, strategic planning, and customer service; he also led the corporate effort to develop the process and systems for deregulating the energy marketplace in New Jersey. Mr. Natale holds a B.S. in civil engineering from Newark College of Engineering and an M.S. in engineering management from the New Jersey Institute of Technology. He completed the Executive Management Program at Yale University and is a licensed professional engineer in New Jersey and a certified association executive.

DIETRAM A. SCHEUFELE is a professor in the Department of Life Sciences Communication and a member of the steering committee of the Robert F. and Jean E. Holtz Center for Science and Technology Studies at the University of Wisconsin (UW)-Madison. He is also the Wisconsin principle investigator of the National Scence Foundation-funded Center for Nanotechnology in Society, located at Arizona State University, and a member of the Nanotechnology Technical Advisory Group to the President's Council of Advisors on Science and Technology. The focus of Dr. Scheufele's research is shaping public attitudes toward science and technology. He has received the Young Scholar Award for outstanding early research from the International Communication Association, the Young Faculty Teaching Excellence Award from the College of Agriculture and Life Sciences at Cornell University, and the Vilas Associate Award from the University of Wisconsin-Madison. His professional experience includes consulting work for major marketing firms and public-sector clients, including the Public Broadcasting System and the World Health Organization. Prior to joining UW in 2004, he was a tenured associate professor and director of graduate studies in the Department of Communication at Cornell University.

JACQUELYN F. SULLIVAN is founding co-director and director of K-12 Engineering Education for the Integrated Teaching and Learning Program at the University of Colorado (CU) at Boulder, a program that is working toward integrating hands-on engineering throughout the K–16 learning experience. In 2008, Sullivan was co-recipient of the National Academy of Engineering Bernard M. Gordon Prize for Innovation in Engineering and Technology Education, and in 2005 she received the inaugural Lifetime Achievement Award from the K–12 Division of the American Society of Engineering Education. Dr. Sullivan had 13 years of engineering and leadership experience in industry prior to joining CU in 1990, and she was instrumental in founding the university's Integrated Teaching and Learning Program, which provides hands-on engineering experience to more than 4,000 undergraduates annually. She also initiated a K–12 engineering education program for teachers and underserved students and is currently leading a multi-institutional initiative to create an online, searchable, standards-based, digital library of K–12 engineering curricula. She heads a U.S. Department of Education and National Science Foundation-funded project, the TEAMS Program (Tomorrow's Engineering—creAte. iMagine. Succeed.) that incorporates weekly hands-on, inquiry-based engineering into engineering and science classes in grades 3 through 12. Dr. Sullivan is a founding board member of the Denver School of Science and Technology—a public, urban high school that incorporates science, engineering, and technology into a humanities-rich setting focused on student achievement. In addition, she is a long-standing member of (and has chaired) the board of directors of a non-profit community school of the arts. She received her Ph.D. in environmental health physics and aquatic toxicology from Purdue University.

B IN-DEPTH INTERVIEWS: INTERVIEWER'S GUIDE

INTRODUCTION

- Explain the idea of the IDI.
- This is being taped so that I don't have to take notes while you are giving your opinions. . . .
- We just want to hear your opinions. . . . There are no right or wrong answers. Just looking for different perspectives.
- Please speak up when you talk. . . .
- If you have any questions or additional comments, please go right ahead at any time. We have a good deal of material to cover in a short time; feel free to ask questions, but we will need to keep the conversation moving. . . .

ENGINEERING

We're working with the National Academy of Engineering, and today we're going to talk about what people think about engineers in general as well as careers in engineering.

- Please tell me a little about what you do in your job.
  - What is your title?
  - How long have you been in your current position?

- What are the first words or phrases that come to mind when you think about 'engineering'? PROBE: Are there any negative words or phrases that come to mind when you think about engineers or engineering?
  - PROBE: What do you think when a young person says he or she wants to become an engineer?

- What kind of person is an engineer? What traits and characteristics does an engineer have? PROBE FOR EXAMPLES

- Thinking back, what was *your* first memorable experience with engineering? With someone who was an engineer? What was that person like?
  - What got you interested in engineering, if you are interested?

- How do you explain engineering to make it more interesting other people? To children?

- FOR ENGINEERS: What prejudices about engineering do you encounter when you tell people you are an engineer?
  - PROBE: What misconceptions do people have about what you and other engineers do?
  - PROBE: How have perceptions about engineering changed since you first became an engineer? IF CHANGED: What caused those opinions to change?
  - PROBE: Do you think engineering and engineers are taken for granted?

- FOR ENGINEERS: What would you like to change about the public's image of engineers and engineering? How would you change it?

- What is *right* with engineering?
- PROBE: What effect does engineering's image have on the long-term health of your profession?

- How do you think engineering is seen as a profession by most people? What image do you think engineering has among school-age children?
  - PROBE: How have perceptions about engineering changed in the last few decades? Have they changed? IF CHANGED: What caused those opinions to change?
  - Where do you see the image of engineering and engineers in ten years? In twenty years? What should it be?
  - What areas of engineering will be more prominent? Chemical, civil, electrical, industrial, manufacturing, mechanical, biochemical? Others? Why? Which will be less prominent? Why?

- Have you seen anything that others have done to promote engineering? PROBE FOR SPECIFICS.

- What do you think *should* be done to promote a more positive image of engineering? What are the specific images or messages about engineering that the field should be emphasizing?
  - What should the field of engineering NOT be promoting? Why not?

- What do you think of others' efforts to cultivate greater public awareness of engineering? PROBE: National Engineers Week? Competitions? Tool kits for teachers and guidance counselors; mentor programs; school-to-work training; cable television shows?
  - PROBE: What do you think has worked? What do you think didn't/doesn't work? How could these efforts be re-directed or made better?
  - PROBE: Are these efforts targeted at the right audiences?

- Why would a child be interested in engineering? What things about engineering do you think could be emphasized to make engineering more appealing to children? To students considering studying engineering at college? To young people considering engineering as a career?
  - What visual images of engineering do you think make engineering more appealing? Which images make engineering less appealing?

- What would you tell a student who asked you about a career in engineering? Where would you send them for more information?
  - What could make a career in engineering more appealing to young people?

- Can you name any engineers who are widely known?
  - PROBE: Who is the face of engineering? Who would be a good spokesperson for engineering?

- What is a good example of engineering at work today? PROBE: What are the success stories that engineering should be telling?
  - Some people say scientists get all the credit for scientific advances, and architects get all the credit for buildings and other projects, but engineers get only the blame when a disaster happens. Do agree that this is the case? Why/why not?

THEMES

- I'd like to ask you about some possible themes that could be used to promote engineering. ROTATE THEMES First...
  - *A LIMITLESS IMAGINATION*: This theme speaks to the innovative, design-driven nature of engineering.

- FOR EACH POSSIBLE THEME, ASK: What do you think of this as a theme to promote engineering?
  - PROBES: What examples should be used to illuminate this theme? What images should be associated with this theme? What examples or images should be avoided?
  - *AN ENTERPRISING SPIRIT*: This theme recognizes the inventive spirit and pioneering contributions of the field.
  - *FREE TO EXPLORE*: This theme evokes the constant journey that is the engineer's quest for new solutions.
  - *IDEAS IN ACTION*: This theme underscores how engineering uniquely bridges the world of science with the real world.
  - PROBE: Is it useful to think of engineers as 'real-world scientists'?
  - *SHAPE THE FUTURE*: This theme speaks to how engineering offers an empowering and rewarding career.
  - *LIFE TAKES ENGINEERING*: This theme focuses on the field's essential role and life-changing work.

- Of the possible themes we discussed, which do you think will be the most effective? Why? Which do you, personally like the best? Why? Which don't you like?

- Can you suggest any other themes like these that could be used to promote engineering? How would it be delivered? At whom would it be targeted? Why?

WRAP UP

- What effect do you think a change in engineering's image would have on the field? How about for you, professionally?

- Finally, if you could give one piece of marketing communications advice to promote engineering, what would it be?

- Is there anything you would like to add that we haven't asked about?

Thank and dismiss.

C FOCUS GROUPS: MODERATOR'S GUIDE—PARENTS

INTRODUCTION **(5 MINUTES)**

- **Moderator introduction:** I represent GSG, an independent opinion-research firm that conducts discussion groups on various topics. We ask people their opinions about everything from hamburgers to cars.

- Explain the idea of the focus group. Go over features of the room, including:
  - One-way mirror—I have colleagues taking notes behind the mirror so that they do not disturb us. . . .
  - Camera/microphones—This is being taped so that I don't have to take notes while you are all giving your opinions. . . . One ground rule: You must talk, and you must talk loud enough so we can all hear you.
  - Completely confidential. Your full names will never be used. We just want to hear your opinions . . . Not a classroom; There are no right or wrong answers.
  - If you have any questions or additional comments, please go right ahead at any time. We have a good deal of material

to cover in a short time; feel free to ask questions, but we will need to keep the conversation moving. . . .

- Group profile: personal background (name, where do you live, how many kids you have and their grades, what you wanted to be when you grew up, etc.).

WARM-UP

- Let's talk a little bit about back when you were in school. What was your favorite subject when you were in high school?
  - PROBE: History/Social Studies, Math, Science, Reading/ English, Foreign Language, Music/Art, Gym?
  - Why did you like that subject?

- What subjects did you like the least? Why?

- Is there a subject that you took in school that, looking back on it, you wish you had learned better? Why do you say that?

- What is your child's favorite subject in school?
  - PROBE: History/Social Studies, Math, Science, Reading/ English, Foreign Language, Music/Art, Gym?
  - How do you think your child ended up liking that subject?

- What subject does your child like the least? Why?

- Do your children know yet what they want to do when they're grown up?
  - What school subjects do you think your children will need to excel in to have a chance to go into their chosen line of work?
  - What subjects do you think your children could do without? Why?

- When you help your child with their schoolwork, what is *your* favorite subject? Why? What is it that you like about that subject?
  - How did you end up liking that subject? Was it because of a certain teacher? A certain project?

- What subject do you *least* enjoy helping your child with? Why?

CAREERS

- Let's talk about your children and how they may choose their careers. What do you think your children want to become when they grow up? Have they already decided what they want to do when they grow up?
  - IF CHOSEN, ASK: Why do you think they have chosen that field? Do you think you will be able to do it? What will they need to do to go into that field?
  - IF NOT CHOSEN, ASK: Why do you think they have yet to choose?

- Think for a moment about some reasons you would want to have a certain kind of job or career. . . . What are some reasons why someone might try to have a certain job or career? GO TO BOARD, WRITE.
  - PROBE: Satisfaction? Celebrity? Recognition (honors, awards)? Interesting work? Money? Good career? Good lifestyle? Challenging? Good opportunities? Able to create things that will last? Competitive?

- Have you ever spoken with your children about what they want to become or what subject he or she wants to study in college?
  - What was this conversation like?
  - How much influence would you say you have on whether your (son or daughter) goes to college?

- Let's think again about when you were growing up. . . . Did you know anyone who had a job that was similar to the one you are doing now?
  - What was that person like?

ENGINEERING

- Now we're going to talk about another topic. . . . Engineering. What are the first words or phrases that come to mind when you think about 'engineering'? WRITE ON BOARD. PROBE FOR AS MANY AS POSSIBLE.
  - PROBE: Are there any positive words or phrases that come to mind when you think about engineers or engineering? How about negative words?

- What kind of person is an engineer? What traits and characteristics does an engineer have? PROBE FOR EXAMPLES.

- Do you know anyone who is an engineer? What does that person do? What is that person like?
  - PROBE: Can you name any engineers who are widely known?

- What are some examples of engineering at work today? WRITE ON BOARD
  - PROBE: What are the most interesting things on this list? Why? What skills would a person need to be able to do those things? What kind of person does those things?

- DISTRIBUTE HANDOUTS: I have something I would like you take a look at. Write your first name and your last initial at the top of the sheet. Here are some examples of engineering at work today. I'd like you to circle the ones you find most interesting or appealing, and cross out the ones you find very boring or least appealing. And when you've circled and crossed out some of the items on the list, I want you to number 1, 2,

3 the three most interesting or appealing of the things on this list.
- – PROBE: What did you pick as the most interesting thing on this list? Why? What skills would a person need to be able to do those things? What kind of person does those things?

- What's the difference between a scientist and an engineer? Is there any difference? What does a scientist do that an engineer doesn't do? What does an engineer do that a scientist doesn't?

- Now I'm going to read you a list of descriptions and I want you to tell me if it's more appropriate for scientists or engineers. . . . We can only give each description away once. . . Would you say scientists or engineers are better described as . . . Designers? Creators? Inventors? Lab technicians? Planners? Leaders? Followers? Original thinkers? Problem solvers? Hard working? Get results? Have a positive effect on people's everyday lives? Innovative? Successful?
  - – PROBE FOR EACH: Why does that describe engineers/ scientists better?

- Some people have said that engineers are 'real-world scientists.' What do you think that means? Do you agree? What does 'real world' mean?

I'd like to ask you about some other things that people have said about engineers and engineering. . . .

- Some people describe engineers as creative problem-solvers. They describe engineers as having a vision for how things should work, and they ask questions like 'how does it work?' 'what will happen if . . . ?' and they work with other smart people to design and build new things and solve problems.

- – PROBE: Is that description appealing to you? What is appealing about that? What are some kinds of examples of that kind of person?

- Some people describe engineers as being free to explore, and looking for better ideas, constantly learning new things, and they are never bored because there are always problems to find that need solving. Engineers are always being challenged and inspired to keep exploring.
  - – PROBE: Is that description appealing to you? What is appealing about that? What are some kinds of examples of that kind of person?

- Some people describe engineers as making a world of difference because they're able to shape the future, have a direct effect on people's everyday lives, and solve tomorrow's problems today.
  - – PROBE: Is that description appealing to you? What is appealing about that? What are some kinds of examples of that kind of person?

- What kind of careers do you think engineers have?
  - – PROBE: How much money do they make? Do they work insane hours? Do they get to travel? Is their work interesting?

- Do you think engineering would be a good career for your child?
  - – RETURN TO LIST OF CAREER ATTRIBUTES ON BOARD, ASK: Does a career in engineering have any of these career attributes?

- I want you to turn your handouts to the last page now. I want you to imagine that you are in charge of a marketing campaign to promote to young people to consider becoming an engineer or studying engineering, and your job is to write a slogan to promote others to consider becoming an engineer. On the second set of lines, I want you to write down what you think the best image or photograph should go with your slogan.

CHECK IN BACK ROOM FOR OTHER QUESTIONS.

WRAP UP

- What did you write for a slogan? What image or photograph did you choose? Why?

Thank and dismiss.

D FOCUS GROUPS: MODERATOR'S GUIDE—TEENS

INTRODUCTION (5 MINUTES)

- **Moderator introduction:** I represent GSG, an independent opinion-research firm that conducts discussion groups on various topics. We ask people their opinions about everything from hamburgers to cars.

- Explain the idea of the focus group. Go over features of the room, including:
  - One-way mirror—I have colleagues taking notes behind the mirror so that they do not disturb us. . . .
  - Camera/Microphones—This is being taped so that I don't have to take notes while you are all giving your opinions. . . . One ground rule: You must talk, and you must talk loud enough so we can all hear you.
  - Completely confidential. Your full names will never be used. We just want to hear your opinions . . . Not a classroom; There are no right or wrong answers.
  - If you have any questions or additional comments, please go right ahead at any time. We have a good deal of material

to cover in a short time; feel free to ask questions, but we will need to keep the conversation moving. . . .

- Introductions: First name (only), and background information (family, favorite subject at school, favorite television show, favorite site on the internet, etc.).

WARM-UP

- You told me what your favorite subject in school is. Tell me why that's your favorite subject.
  - What is it that you like about that subject? If you were trying to explain to someone else why they might like that subject, what would you tell them?
  - How did you end up liking that subject? Was it because of a certain teacher? A certain project?

- Now, what is your *least* favorite subject in school?
  - PROBE: History/Social Studies, Math, Science, Reading/English, Foreign Language, Music/Art, Gym?

- Let's talk about what your plans are, and ask a question you've probably been asked a few times. . . . What do you want to do when you grow up?
  - Why do you want to do that? Do you think you will be able to do it?

- Think for a moment about some reasons you would want to have a certain kind of job or career… What are some reasons why someone might try to have a certain job or career? GO TO BOARD, WRITE.
  - PROBE: Satisfaction? Celebrity? Recognition (honors, awards)? Interesting work? Money? Good career? Good lifestyle? Challenging? Good opportunities? Able to create things that will last? Competitive?

- Do you know anyone who has a job now that you would like to have yourself when you are older?
  - What is that person like? Why did that person succeed in making that career for themselves? What did that person do to get where they are?

- What school subjects do you think you will need to excel in to have a chance to go into your chosen line of work? Why? How do you like those subjects? Why?
  - What subjects in school do you think you could do without? Why?

- Have you ever spoken with an adult about what you want to become? Who did you talk to? PROBE: A parent? A teacher or a guidance counselor? A family friend?
  - What was this conversation like? Why did you seek that particular person out?

- Now we're going to talk about another topic. . . . Engineering. What are the first words or phrases that come to mind when you think about 'engineering'? WRITE ON BOARD. PROBE FOR AS MANY AS POSSIBLE.
  - PROBE: Are there any positive words or phrases that come to mind when you think about engineers or engineering? How about negative words?

- What kind of person is an engineer? What traits and characteristics does an engineer have? PROBE FOR EXAMPLES.

- Do you know anyone who is an engineer? What does that person do? What is that person like?
  - PROBE: Can you name any engineers who are widely known?

- What are some examples of engineering at work today? WRITE ON BOARD.

- – PROBE: What are the most interesting things on this list? Why? What skills would a person need to be able to do those things? What kind of person does those things?

- DISTRIBUTE HANDOUTS. I have something I would like you take a look at. Write your first name and your last initial at the top of the sheet. Here are some examples of engineering at work today. I'd like you to circle the ones you find most interesting or appealing, and cross out the ones you find very boring or least appealing. And when you've circled and crossed out some of the items on the list, I want you to number 1, 2, 3 the three most interesting or appealing of the things on this list.
  - – PROBE: What did you pick as the most interesting thing on this list? Why? What skills would a person need to be able to do those things? What kind of person does those things?

- What's the difference between a scientist and an engineer? Is there any difference? What does a scientist do that an engineer doesn't do? What does an engineer do that a scientist doesn't?

- Now I'm going to read you a list of descriptions and I want you to tell me if it's more appropriate for scientists or engineers. . . . We can only give each description away once. . . Would you say scientists or engineers are better described as . . . Designers? Creators? Inventors? Lab technicians? Planners? Leaders? Followers? Original thinkers? Problem-solvers? Hard working? Get results? Have a positive effect on people's everyday lives? Innovative? Successful?
  - – PROBE FOR EACH: Why does that describe engineers/ scientists better?

- Some people have said that engineers are 'real-world scientists.' What do you think that means? Do you agree? What does 'real world' mean?

I'd like to ask you about some other things that people have said about engineers and engineering....

- Some people describe engineers as creative problem solvers. They describe engineers as having a vision for how things should work, and they ask questions like 'how does it work?' 'what will happen if . . . ?' and they work with other smart people to design and build new things and solve problems.
  - PROBE: Is that description appealing to you? What is appealing about that? What are some kinds of examples of that kind of person?

- Some people describe engineers as being free to explore, and looking for better ideas, constantly learning new things, and they are never bored because there are always problems to find that need solving. Engineers are always being challenged and inspired to keep exploring.
  - PROBE: Is that description appealing to you? What is appealing about that? What are some kinds of examples of that kind of person?

- Some people describe engineers as making a world of difference because they're able to shape the future, have a direct effect on people's everyday lives, and solve tomorrow's problems today.
  - PROBE: Is that description appealing to you? What is appealing about that? What are some kinds of examples of that kind of person?

- What kind of careers do you think engineers have?
  - PROBE: How much money do they make? Do they work insane hours? Do they get to travel? Is their work interesting?

- I want you to turn your handouts to the last page now. I want you to imagine that you are in charge of a marketing campaign to promote to other young people to consider becoming an engineer or studying engineering, and your job is to write a slogan to promote others to consider becoming an engineer. On the second set of lines, I want you to write down what you think is the best image or photograph that should go with your slogan.

CHECK IN BACK ROOM FOR OTHER QUESTIONS.

WRAP UP

- What did you write for a slogan? What image or photograph did you choose? Why?

Thank and dismiss.

E YOUTH TRIADS: MODERATOR'S GUIDE

INTRODUCTION

- Explain the idea of the group. Go over features of the room, including:
- Camera/microphones—This is being taped so that I don't have to take notes while you are giving your opinions. . . .
- One-way mirror—I have colleagues behind the mirror taking notes so that they do not disturb us. . . .
- This is not a classroom; and I am not a teacher; there are no wrong answers.
- Completely confidential. Your full names will never be used. We just want to hear your opinions. . . . There are no right or wrong answers.
- The microphone overhead. Please speak up when you talk so that we can all hear you.
- Even though you know each other and are friends, please be sure to let everyone say what he has to say. Please don't talk over one another.
- If you have any questions or additional comments, please go right ahead at any time. . . .

WARM-UP

To begin, I'd like to talk about you...

- First tell me a little about yourself, your name, where you live, where you go to school, and what your LEAST favorite subject in school is. . . .
  - PROBE: History/Social Studies, Math, Science, Reading/English, Foreign Language, Music/Art, Gym?
  - PROBE: Why don't you like that subject?

- How long have you been friends? How did you meet each other?

- You told me what your favorite subject in school is. Tell me why that's your favorite subject.
  - What is it that you like about that subject? If you were trying to explain to someone else why they might like that subject, what would you tell them?
  - How did you end up liking that subject? Was it because of a certain teacher? A certain project?

- Have you ever taken a field trip or done a school project that you really enjoyed? Tell me about one good trip you took or project that you did. If it was fun, what made it fun? What did you learn?

CAREERS

- What do you want to do when you grow up?
  - Why do you want to do that? Do you think you will be able to do it?

- Do you know anyone who has a job now that you would like to have yourself when you are older?
  - What is that person like? Why did that person succeed in making that career for themselves? What did that person do to get where they are?

- Have you ever spoken with your mother or father or another adult about what you want to become when you grow up? Who did you talk to? PROBE: A parent? A teacher? A family friend?
  - What was this conversation like? Why did you talk to that person?

ENGINEERING

- Now we're going to talk about another topic… Engineering and engineers. I want you to write down for me what an engineer is and a few things about what an engineer does. What is an engineer? HAVE EACH CHILD WRITE DEFINITION AND DESCRIPTION.
  - What did you write? Why?
  - What kind of person is an engineer? PROBE FOR EXAMPLES.

- What kind of things do engineers do? Are there things that engineers do that you would like to do?
  - Are there activities that engineers do that you don't like or wouldn't want to do?
  - What do you think your friends would say if you told them you wanted to become an engineer?

- Do you know anyone who is an engineer? What does that person do? What is that person like?

VISUALS

- Now I'm going to show you some pictures of some different activities that engineers do. I'd like you each to pick two that you like or that you would like to do. **SPREAD PICTURES OUT ON TABLE.**

- Why did you pick those two images? **PROBE:** Have you done that activity before?
  - Why? What skills would a person need to be able to do those things? What kind of person does those things?

- **FOLLOW UP TO VISUALS:** Have you ever designed anything? Have you ever worked together with a team to solve a problem? Have you ever built anything? Have you ever done a science experiment? Have you ever written a computer program? Have you ever been on a construction site? Done a chemistry experiment? Built a model plane?

WAYS OF TALKING ABOUT ENGINEERING

I'm going to tell you a little about engineers and what they do, and, afterwards, I want you to tell me what you think. . . .

- Some people describe engineers as creative problem-solvers. They describe engineers as having a vision for how things should work, and they ask questions like 'how does it work?' 'what will happen if . . . ?' and they work with other smart people to design and build new things and solve problems.
  - What do you think? What's the first thing you think of after hearing that description? Is that what you think engineers are? What is creative problem solving?

- Some people describe engineers as being free to explore, and looking for better ideas, constantly learning new things, and they are never bored because there are always problems that need solving. Engineers are always being challenged and inspired to keep exploring.
  - What do you think? What's the first thing you think of after hearing that description? Is that what you think engineers are? What is exploring? What does it mean to be free to explore?

- Some people describe engineers as making a difference because they're able to help people by creating things that people will use, and have a direct effect on other people's everyday lives.
  - What do you think? What's the first thing you think of after hearing that description? Is that what you think engineers are? What does it mean to have a direct effect on people's everyday lives?

- Does engineering sound like something you would want to do?
  - Why? Why not?

WRAP UP

MODERATOR CHECKS BACK IN VIEWING ROOM FOR ANY ADDITIONAL QUESTIONS.

I just have a few more questions. . . .

Thank and dismiss.

F   ONLINE SURVEY

GLOBAL STRATEGY GROUP
WWW.GLOBALSTRATEGYGROUP.COM

Copyright   December 2006   500 Adults
Online Survey FINAL   400 14-16 year olds

(INTRO)

Thank you for taking the time to participate in this online survey research project, which is sponsored by the National Academies, a non-governmental organization concerned with such issues as education, employment in scientific and technical fields, and the country's economic health. The answers you give will help the National Academies better understand how to address some of the challenges facing the United States. Your responses will be combined with those of other survey participants, and only those grouped responses will be shared with the National Academies. In other words, no one will know your individual responses to the survey questions.

To begin...
(INFORMED ADULTS SCREENER)
XI102. What is the last grade that you completed in school?

1.	Some grade school	TERMINATE
2.	Some high school	TERMINATE
3.	Graduated high school	TERMINATE
4.	Technical/Vocational	TERMINATE
5.	Some college	CONTINUE
6.	Graduated college	CONTINUE
7.	Graduate professional	CONTINUE

XI102. Generally speaking, how much attention do you follow the news, including what's happening local, statewide, or nationally -- a great deal, some, a little, not very much?

1. A great deal
2. Some
3. A little
4. Not very much
5. Not at all

XI103. Generally speaking, how involved are you in your community as a volunteer -- a great deal, some, a little, not very much?

1. Very involved
2. Somewhat involved
3. A little involved
4. Not very involved
5. Not involved at all

TERMINATE IF PUNCH 3-5 IN BOTH XI102 AND XI103

NEW YORK   WASHINGTON DC   CONNECTICUT   ARKANSAS
895 BROADWAY, 5TH FLOOR 4445 WILLARD AVENUE, SUITE 1040 36 TRUMBULL STREET, 3RD FLOOR THREE FINANCIAL CENTRE
NEW YORK, NY 10003   CHEVY CHASE, MD 20815   HARTFORD, CT 06103   900 SOUTH SHACKLEFORD, SUITE 510
212.260.8813   301.951.5200   860.547.1414   LITTLE ROCK, AR 72211
212.260.9058 FAX   301.951.7040 FAX   860.548.0842 FAX   501.954.7878 FAX 501.954.9955

(ADULTS SCREENER)

XA1.   Are you eighteen years of age or over?

    1.   Yes   **CONTINUE**
    2.   No   **TERMINATE**
    3.   Don't know/Refused   **TERMINATE**

XA2.   For each of the following professions or careers someone just starting out in the work world may choose, please indicate whether you think it would be a very good choice, a good choice, a fair choice, or a bad choice as a career or profession.
(SCRAMBLE CHOICES)

	Very Good Choice	Good Choice	Fair Choice	Bad Choice
Teacher	☐	☐	☐	☐
Doctor	☐	☐	☐	☐
Engineer	☐	☐	☐	☐
Lawyer	☐	☐	☐	☐
Architect	☐	☐	☐	☐
Scientist	☐	☐	☐	☐

(TEENS SCREENER)

XT1.   Are you between the ages of 14 and 17 years of age?

    1.   Yes   **CONTINUE**
    2.   No   **TERMINATE**
    3.   Don't know/Refused   **TERMINATE**

XT2.   When you graduate high school, how likely is it that you will attend college?

    1.   Definitely will attend college
    2.   Probably will attend college
    3.   Chances are 50-50
    4.   Probably not
    5.   Definitely not

XT3.   For each of the following professions or careers someone like yourself may choose, please indicate whether you think it would be a very good choice, a good choice, a fair choice, or a bad choice as a career or profession.
(SCRAMBLE CHOICES)

	Very Good Choice	Good Choice	Fair Choice	Bad Choice
Teacher	☐	☐	☐	☐
Doctor	☐	☐	☐	☐
Engineer	☐	☐	☐	☐
Lawyer	☐	☐	☐	☐
Architect	☐	☐	☐	☐
Scientist	☐	☐	☐	☐

(MAIN SURVEY)

1.   Please indicate how important each of the following is [(FOR TEENS) to you] /[(FOR ADULTS) should be to someone starting a career] in considering which career to get into. (SCRAMBLE CHOICES)

	Extremely important	Very important	Somewhat important	Not that important	Not important at all
Salary	☐	☐	☐	☐	☐
Recognition	☐	☐	☐	☐	☐
Interesting Work	☐	☐	☐	☐	☐
Challenging Work	☐	☐	☐	☐	☐
Work that makes a difference, is meaningful	☐	☐	☐	☐	☐
Availability of jobs in the field	☐	☐	☐	☐	☐
Prestigious field	☐	☐	☐	☐	☐

2.   On the following one to ten scale, with ten being you know very well what a person in this profession does day-to-day and one being you don't know at all what a person in this profession does day-to-day, please rate your knowledge of each profession. (SCRAMBLE CHOICES)

	10 – Know very well	9	8	7	6	5	4	3	2	1 – Don't know at all
Teacher	☐	☐	☐	☐	☐	☐	☐	☐	☐	☐
Doctor	☐	☐	☐	☐	☐	☐	☐	☐	☐	☐
Engineer	☐	☐	☐	☐	☐	☐	☐	☐	☐	☐
Lawyer	☐	☐	☐	☐	☐	☐	☐	☐	☐	☐
Architect	☐	☐	☐	☐	☐	☐	☐	☐	☐	☐
Scientist	☐	☐	☐	☐	☐	☐	☐	☐	☐	☐

3.   Thinking about the field of engineering… what words come to mind when you see or hear the word ENGINEERING? (OPEN END)

_____

_____

4. For each of the following, please indicate how well you think it describes engineers or the field of engineering. (SPLIT SAMPLE)
(SCRAMBLE CHOICES)

Describes engineers or the engineering profession…

	Very well	Somewhat well	Not very well	Not well at all
Creative	☐	☐	☐	☐
The work is rewarding	☐	☐	☐	☐
Fun	☐	☐	☐	☐
Get results	☐	☐	☐	☐
Hard working	☐	☐	☐	☐
Have a positive effect on people's everyday lives	☐	☐	☐	☐
Inventors	☐	☐	☐	☐
Leaders	☐	☐	☐	☐
Nerdy	☐	☐	☐	☐
Original thinkers	☐	☐	☐	☐
Problem solvers	☐	☐	☐	☐
Well-paid	☐	☐	☐	☐
Must be smart to get into this field	☐	☐	☐	☐
Must be good at math and science	☐	☐	☐	☐
Builds, constructs and makes things	☐	☐	☐	☐
Designs, draws and plans things	☐	☐	☐	☐
Sits at a desk all day	☐	☐	☐	☐
Mostly men	☐	☐	☐	☐
Mostly white	☐	☐	☐	☐
Well-respected	☐	☐	☐	☐
Requires too many years of school to get a degree	☐	☐	☐	☐
Entrepreneurial	☐	☐	☐	☐
Boring	☐	☐	☐	☐
Often work outdoors	☐	☐	☐	☐

5. For the following examples of engineering, please indicate how appealing it is. In other words, how well does it create interest for you in engineering? If you don't think it is a good example of engineering, please indicate that. (SPLIT SAMPLE) (SCRAMBLE)

	4 – Very appealing	3	2	1 – Not appealing at all	Not good example
Space exploration	☐	☐	☐	☐	☐
Designing video games	☐	☐	☐	☐	☐
Building an acoustically-perfect concert hall	☐	☐	☐	☐	☐
Designing the world's fastest plane	☐	☐	☐	☐	☐
Developing new foods	☐	☐	☐	☐	☐
Creating more advanced M.R.I. machines to do better brain and body scans to diagnose health problems	☐	☐	☐	☐	☐
D.N.A. testing	☐	☐	☐	☐	☐
Using D.N.A. evidence to solve crimes	☐	☐	☐	☐	☐
Building cars that run on alternative fuels	☐	☐	☐	☐	☐
Making cars safer	☐	☐	☐	☐	☐
Growing organs for transplants	☐	☐	☐	☐	☐
Making smaller, faster computer processors	☐	☐	☐	☐	☐
Protecting the rainforest by developing new ways to farm that don't require so much land	☐	☐	☐	☐	☐
Developing new fabrics	☐	☐	☐	☐	☐
Protecting the water supply	☐	☐	☐	☐	☐
Missile defense systems	☐	☐	☐	☐	☐
Smart traffic solutions	☐	☐	☐	☐	☐
High-definition television	☐	☐	☐	☐	☐
Building the world's longest bridge	☐	☐	☐	☐	☐
iPod	☐	☐	☐	☐	☐
Wind power	☐	☐	☐	☐	☐
Making homes safer	☐	☐	☐	☐	☐
Velcro	☐	☐	☐	☐	☐
Reducing air pollution	☐	☐	☐	☐	☐
Turning deserts into farmland	☐	☐	☐	☐	☐
Solar energy	☐	☐	☐	☐	☐
Machines that allow blind people to see	☐	☐	☐	☐	☐

6.   Next you will read some statements that people have made about engineering. After you read each statement, please answer the questions below. (STATEMENTS SCRAMBLED)

a.   Engineers are creative problem-solvers. They have a vision for how something should work, and are dedicated to making it better, faster or more efficient.
b.   Engineers connect science to the real world. They collaborate with scientists and other specialists (such as animators, architects or chemists) to turn bold new ideas into reality.
c.   Engineering is essential to our health, happiness and safety. From the grandest skyscrapers to microscopic medical devices, it is impossible to imagine life without engineering.
d.   Engineers help shape the future. They use the latest science, tools and technology to bring ideas to life.
e.   Engineers make a world of difference. From new farming equipment and safer drinking water to electric cars and faster microchips, engineers use their knowledge to improve people's lives in meaningful ways.

Qa.   How appealing this statement is to you, personally?

   1.   Not appealing at all
   2.   Not that appealing
   3.   Somewhat appealing
   4.   Very appealing

Qb.   How believable is this statement?

   1.   Not at all believable
   2.   Not that believable
   3.   Somewhat believable
   4.   Very believable

Qc.   How much do you, personally, care about what this statement says and the examples included in it?

   1.   Do not care at all
   2.   Don't care that much
   3.   Care somewhat
   4.   Care very much

7.   And of these statements, which is most appealing to you, personally? (STATEMENTS SCRAMBLED)

a.   Engineers are creative problem-solvers. They have a vision for how something should work, and are dedicated to making it better, faster or more efficient.
b.   Engineers connect science to the real world. They collaborate with scientists and other specialists (such as animators, architects or chemists) to turn bold new ideas into reality.

    c. Engineering is essential to our health, happiness and safety. From the grandest skyscrapers to microscopic medical devices, it is impossible to imagine life without engineering.

    d. Engineers help shape the future. They use the latest science, tools and technology to bring ideas to life.

    e. Engineers make a world of difference. From new farming equipment and safer drinking water to electric cars and faster microchips, engineers use their knowledge to improve people's lives in meaningful ways.

8.   And of these statements, which is <u>least</u> appealing to you, personally?
         (STATEMENTS SCRAMBLED IN SAME ORDER AS IN Q.7)

9.   The following are some taglines or slogans that might be used to describe engineering. Please indicate how appealing that tagline or slogan is to you, personally.
         SCALE TO CODE:
         1.   Not appealing at all
         2.   Not that appealing
         3.   Somewhat appealing
         4.   Very appealing

         (SLOGANS OR TAGLINES SCRAMBLED) (WILL APPEAR AS LIST ON SCREEN)

         a.   Bolder by design.
         b.   Because dreams need doing.
         c.   Turning ideas into reality.
         d.   Life takes engineering.
         e.   The power to do.
         f.   Behind the next big thing.
         g.   Designed to work wonders.

The following questions are for statistical purposes only.
ADULT
A101.   What is your age?

         1.   18-24
         2.   25-29
         3.   30-34
         4.   35-39
         5.   40-44
         6.   45-49
         7.   50-54
         8.   55-59
         9.   60-64
         10.   65-69
         11.   70+

TEEN
T101. What is your age?

    1.   14
    2.   15
    3.   16
    4.   17

ADULT
A102. What is the last grade that you completed in school?

    1.   Some grade school
    2.   Some high school
    3.   Graduated high school
    4.   Technical/Vocational
    5.   Some college
    6.   Graduated college
    7.   Graduate professional

ADULT
A107. Do you currently have any children under 18 living at home with you?

    1.   Yes
    2.   No

ADULT
A108. What is your current or most recent occupation?
      (OPEN END)

D300. And just to make sure we have a representative sample of Americans, could you please tell me your race? (ACCEPT MULTIPLE RESPONSES)

    1.   Black/African-American
    2.   White/Caucasian
    3.   Hispanic/Latino
    4.   Asian-American
    5.   Other

D100. Gender

    1.   Male
    2.   Female

D400. STATE

Praise for *A People's History of Chicago*

"I just read your new manuscript and got the same feeling I had some weeks ago when I was back in Chicago in a cab very early in the morning on my way to catch a train, the city shrouded in a misty rain, and as we passed what has always been one of my favorite historic intersections by the river at michigan and wacker (where once long long ago the freshly created soul of jazz poured out of the London House) there was this fucking sign, TRUMP, like an obscenity scrawled across chicago history, illuminated like a raw scar. There's that sense to your book, the scars of how the city was made are part of the architecture, of the landscape."
—Stuart Dybek, author of *The Coast of Chicago*,
recipient of a MacArthur Foundation Fellowship

"The stories and personalities memorialized in these poems are real to me. Poet Kevin Coval breathes them back alive with word-pictures both concrete and passionate, compressing centuries into verse. These are poems to be savored. I'd be hard-pressed to pick just one favorite from this remarkable collection."
—Timuel D. Black, Chicago historian/activist/teacher, author of
Bridges of Memory: Chicago's First Wave of Black Migration

"Kevin Coval has given us a gift, a collection of heartfelt, piercing poems, stories really, about America's city. Taken together, these song-like postcards are a kind of celebration, as well as some takedowns, of those who sweat and struggle and endure to make this city a better place. The book soars."
—Alex Kotlowitz, author of *There Are No Children Here* and *Never a City So Real*

"From our first resident, Jean Baptiste Point du Sable, to the immigrants, migrants, and souls who make this city great, a vibrant, dynamic collection of vignettes that expose the naked truth of our fair city."
—Karen Lewis, teacher and president of the Chicago Teachers Union, Local 1

"Kevin Coval is a dazzling, dizzying time traveler and cultural historian-poet. He is a lover of language, rhythms, and colors and the people who transform in these. He knows the stories of Chicago and all its people—Red, Black, White, Brown, Asian, Queer, Straight. The spine of this book is the people's resistance and struggle for justice and a fair shake. But—not to worry—Kevin puts it all to you so sweetly, so energetically, so for real—he makes you smile behind poem after poem. And then again he makes you want to rise up. He's in the Chicago tradition—fire, earth, and endless blues."
—Angela Jackson, author of *Where I Must Go*,
winner of the American Book Award

"An epic that is both intimate and sweeping... Coval's poems not only bridge the past and the present; they create a community through history, returning the city to those who built and continue to build it."
—Lovia Gyarkye, *New Republic*

"A masterpiece."   —Haki Madhubuti, cofounder of Third World Press

"A fascinating book of beautiful poems."   —Trevor Noah, *The Daily Show*

"Coval's book pays homage to Howard Zinn's beloved *A People's History of the United States* not just in its name but also in its defiantly radical spirit."
                   —*Chicago Reader*

"Big and inviting, direct and accessible, *A People's History of Chicago* is a passionate and illuminating collection. Reading Coval's words evokes the experience of being guided through the city by someone who loves it for what it is and pushes it toward the potential of what it could become."
                   —Kathleen Rooney, *Chicago Tribune*

"A magnificent, important, affectionate, and blistering book... Coval's poems capture the city so powerfully that they beg favorable comparison with another Chicago-defining book of poems published a century ago, Carl Sandburg's *Chicago Poems*."   —Rick Kogan, *Chicago Tribune*

"Chicago is a collision of art and politics, oppression and liberation, workers and immigrants, activism and organizing, La Villita and the Black Metropolis. With *A People's History of Chicago*, Coval resurrects our history and brings this great American city to life with all of its scars and bruises, its sparkling beauty, its broken noses, cut lips, and contradictions intact."   —Bill Ayers, *Truthout*

"Kevin Coval clears the smoke with the real and sometimes forgotten stories of Chicago's working-class heroes."   —*Chicago Sun-Times*

"In history, there is the official narrative, and there is the parallel, underreported version of events. There's the Great Man interpretation of our collective past, and there's the view from the grassroots. Kevin Coval's *A People's History of Chicago* is an alternate chronology of the city he calls home. The book is animated by a twin desire to celebrate the contributions of working people and the endless cultural stamina of Chicago's minority communities."   —*Chicagoist*

"Invoking past Chicago writers and artists like Studs Terkel, Gwendolyn Brooks, and Common, Coval joins those who so engrossed themselves in their city that they found a mirror reflection of the beauty and horror of the entire country within its confines."   —*Los Angeles Review of Books*

"Chicago is under indictment for gun violence, police brutality, and racial segregation, but it is also a city of poets—Carl Sandburg and Gwendolyn Brooks most famously. With this agile, wryly funny, righteous, and passionate book, Kevin Coval adds his clarion hip-hop voice to the chorus."   —Donna Seaman, *Booklist*

"Kevin Coval has composed a heartfelt song for his hometown and a trenchant account of its injustices."   —*Publishers Weekly*

A
PEOPLE'S
HISTORY
OF
CHICAGO

✴ ✴ ✴ ✴

Kevin Coval

Chicago, Illinois
Haymarket Books

Published in 2017 by
Haymarket Books
P.O. Box 180165
Chicago, IL 60618
773-583-7884
www.haymarketbooks.org
info@haymarketbooks.org

ISBN: 978-1-60846-671-9

Trade distribution:
In the US, Consortium Book Sales and Distribution, www.cbsd.com
In Canada, Publishers Group Canada, www.pgcbooks.ca
In the UK, Turnaround Publisher Services, www.turnaround-uk.com
All other countries, Publishers Group Worldwide, www.pgw.com

This book was published with the generous support of Lannan Foundation and
    Wallace Action Fund.

Cover design by Brett Nieman. Cover photograph by Bob Simpson of a July
2016 sit-in and march against police violence initiated by four teenage women,
which was punctuated by periods of silence and performances of poetry.

Printed in Canada by union labor.

Library of Congress Cataloging-in-Publication data is available.

10 9 8 7 6 5 4 3 2

If history is to be creative, to anticipate a possible future without denying the past, it should, I believe, emphasize new possibilities by disclosing those hidden episodes of the past when, even if in brief flashes, people showed their ability to resist, to join together, occasionally to win.
—Howard Zinn, *A People's History of the United States*

Contents

Foreword by Chance the Rapper   ix
Shikaakwa   1
lasalle Wrote It Down Wrong   2
The Father Is a Black Man   4
The Treaty of Chicago   6
Hog Butcher for the World   7
Albert Parsons Can Hang   9
How to Be Down   10
The L Gets Open   11
The white City   12
Eugene Debs Reads Marx in Prison   13
Reversing the Flow of the Chicago River   14
The Great Migration   15
The Eastland Disaster   16
The Murder of Eugene Williams   18
Society for Human Rights (America's First Gay Rights Organization) 19
Thomas Dorsey, Gospel's Daddy   21
Gwendolyn Brooks Stands in the Mecca   23
Hansberry vs. Lee   26
Muddy Waters Goes Electric   28
Nelson Algren Meets Simone de Beauvoir at the Palmer House   29
Pickle with a Peppermint Stick   31
Sun Ra Becomes a Synthesizer   33
hugh hefner, a Play Boy   34
Mamie Till Bears the Movement   35
king daley Unfurls His burnham Plan   36
The Division Street Riots   37
Martin Luther King Prays in Marquette Park   38
Studs Terkel Drops a Mixtape   40
Carl Sandburg Village (Where My Parents Met)   41
Wall of Respect   43
AfriCOBRA   44
The Assassination of Chairman Fred Hampton   46
Don L. Lee Becomes Haki Madhubuti   48
The Chicago 21 Plan   49
Leaving Aldine   50
Ode to Steppin   51
Disco Demolition   52
mayor byrne Moves Into & Out of Cabrini Green   54
Ron Hardy Plays the Record Backwards   56

The Assassination of Rudy Lozano   58

Marc Smith Invents the Poetry Slam   59

Collateral Damage   61

The Day Harold Died   63

Patronage   64

Fresh to Death   66

Molemen Beat Tapes   67

Graffiti Blasters: An Erasure (A Buff)   69

The Violent Crime Control & Law Enforcement Act   70

The Etymology of Chicago Joe   71

Common's Resurrection   73

The Supreme Court Makes Color Illegal   74

Erasing the Green   75

Ida B. Wells Testifies in the Ghost Town   77

How to Teach Poetry in Chicago Public Schools   79

Lenard Clark Pedals for Air   81

Baby Come On: An Ode to Footwork   83

A Moratorium on the Death Penalty   85

Praise the House Party   87

Día de las Madres   89

Kanye Says What's on Everybody's Mind   91

I Wasn't in Grant Park when Obama Was Elected   93

Republic Windows Workers Sit In   94

The Night the Modern Wing Was Bombed   95

When King Louie First Heard the Word *Chiraq*   97

An Elegy for Dr. Margaret Burroughs   100

A Dedication to the Inaugural Poet   103

Memoir of the Red X   105

Chief Keef's Epiphany at Lollapalooza   107

Teachers' Strike in the Chicago Tradition   108

During Ramadan the Gates of Heaven Are Open   110

Ms. Devine Explains the Meaning of Modern Art: A Found Poem   112

Two Cities Celebrate Independence Day   113

We Charge Genocide   115

Atoning for the Neo-liberal in All
     or rahm emanuel as the Chicken on Kapparot   116

400 Days   119

The Night the Cubs Win the World Series   122

Chicago Has My Heart   124

Notes   129

Illustration Credits   131

Acknowledgments   133

Foreword

We got the cheat codes.

There's no other place on earth where you can go to a centralized space and see thirteen-, fourteen-, fifteen-, sixteen-, seventeen-, and eighteen-year-olds who want to conquer art and music. I left Chicago for a little and went to LA. But have you ever seen a raw-ass tree or a raw-ass plant that's beautiful, that's fully bloomed and growing? It can't fully bloom if you uproot it. If you take it somewhere else, out of its natural environment, it's not gonna grow the same way. If you take a tree out of the dirt, a Christmas tree, and move it into your crib, it'll stay that exact same tree for a little while before it starts to wilt, but it won't grow anymore. You can't uproot a plant. You have to let it grow. If I were to have grown in LA, I might've grown into some shit I'm not supposed to be or just not grown at all, or just peaked. I can reach my peak in Chicago cuz that's where I was planted and where I can continue to grow.

I had planned on living in LA, but when I was out there going to parties and feeling that vibe, I thought it was ungodly, it wasn't true to who I was born to be or what I was supposed to grow to be. Being there made me realize this is not where I'm supposed to get my biggest experiences. As sad as I ever was in LA, the lowest I've ever been, it's not where my lowest was supposed to be. The highest I've been, the happiest I've been in Los Angeles, was not where my life's happiest moments were supposed to be. Being happy means doing what you are supposed to do, being exactly who you are supposed to be. My god, my inner understanding, whatever it is that guides me, had me recognizing that I'm not supposed to be there.

We have a head start. If you've been in that building once, in the Harold Washington Library, one time, you know. Harold Washington. The first Black mayor of Chicago. A very powerful man. A very connected man. A very humble and grounded man. A household name who died in office while at work. His library is in the center of downtown, in the center of the Loop, where all the trains meet. For us to walk into that building is astounding. My dad volunteered for Harold Washington. That's how he got his record expunged. That's how he dodged the system. Years later, he has a library named after him and I could walk in from the cold and experience this temple.

From the age of fourteen, I was trying to go against the grain, to grow into a time and period where it's dope to be anti-establishment, where it's dope to not just accept all the answers that are given to you but to look for your own answers. I am trying to push that. I'm trying to push that to other people who didn't get taught that. As kids that grew up in the '90s and early 2000s, we are able to ask questions like *What's going on? Who are the people leading us? Who are those people teaching us? What are they telling us? How are they able to tell us that? Who are they and where are they coming from and is it the truth?* I've been taught to be a critical thinker, and I was able to say this doesn't feel right. Having the understanding I've been blessed with, I've been able to discern that that shit is not right, that it doesn't feel right, that it doesn't seem right.

I met Kevin Coval at an orientation at Jones College Prep, the first time I ever went into my high school cuz I didn't check it out beforehand. I just signed up for it and applied. So my first time going up to the school was for the Louder Than A Bomb team orientation and Kevin was doing a writing workshop. Though I didn't make my slam team or to Louder Than A Bomb, Kevin ended up being very instrumental to me.

Kevin Coval is my artistic father. He mentored my friends Malcolm London and Dimress Dunnigan and Fatimah Warner and got me shows, and those shows got me a little bit of bread and the confidence to continue and take the craft seriously. In a lot of ways he was the other side of Brother Mike for me, and anybody from Chicago knows what that means and how big a statement that is. He was that for me and for a lot of people.

Kevin made art a job to me. He made me feel like it was real. He made me feel like the competition was real. He made me feel that the money was real. He made me feel that the love and the fans were real. And if I didn't have him in my life I would've been complacent. He took me out of that space and made me understand what it is to be a poet, what it is to be an artist, and what it is to serve the people.

Chance the Rapper
Chance the Chicagoan

Shikaakwa
before 1492

sea of tall grass. sky quiet
enough to hear yourself think.
ancestors talk shit where the wind
whips brisk from the lake. the face
of the river ripples. land of marsh.
before the steel plow
& forced removal

                    this was *shikaakwa*:

wild leek, onion, garlic. a great
trade center, hundreds of tribes
canoed to the portage to barter fish
& skins, squash & bone, mix languages
& blood: home of Chippewa, Potawatomi
Kickapoo, Ho-Chunk, Ottawa, Miami, Ioway
Sauk, Fox, Blackhawk, Odawa & Illinois.

thousands of years before joliet, lasalle
daley, podmajersky, before tribes were razed,
lakes polluted, the blood diseased, the people
rounded into prisons, reservations, Maywood.

there were ash trees, elms & basswood, oak
hickory. history was stories your elders sang.
the young danced rain & memory awake.
there were thousands, before. this land, a sacred
burial ground, a people we delete.
                              quiet

before your morning paper
put your ear to the earth
hear the terror of the horses
the wails of the hunters
howling in this city of wind
on this land of skunk, the stench
of blood inescapable.

1

lasalle Wrote It Down Wrong
· 1687

gringoed the whole place.
every street & building some flat
mispronunciation, some misshapen
mouth   some murder.

Chicagua wild
garlic in indigenous
utterance.   some funk
music.   some rampant weed
returning, perennial & persistent.

Chicago is malignant, a mass
of machinery built upon mass graves.
the beginning of a long death march.
an inadequate water
down. an erasure, an eraser
pink as the whiteman's tongue.

The Father Is a Black Man
1779

> *There is not a single street in the city of Chicago named in honor of the Black man*
> *who founded this city, not an alley...but John Kinzie, a white man, who came after*
> *DuSable, when DuSable was forced out or pushed out or whatever, he ended up*
> *with DuSable's property, and Kinzie has a bridge, Kinzie has a street, Kinzie has a*
> *building, and all he did was buy DuSable's house.*
> **Lerone Bennett, Jr.**

the father is mixed. the father is Black.
his mother a slave. his father a french
mariner. the first non-Native
to settle in Chicago
Jean Baptiste Point duSable
was a hustler.
he worked the trap.
traded pelts at the frontier.
married Kittihawa
a Potawatomi woman
he saw sailing the Mississippi.
the traditional ceremony
officiated by a Chief.
the father was cool
with the Indigenous.
they settled at the mouth
of the river, where the tribune sits
spewing untruths in english.
DuSable spoke spanish, french, english
& several Native dialects.
the father a genius.

he made okra & oxtails
with sos pwa noir, a black bean
sauce, & joumou, a pumpkin stew
harvested from the acres he farmed.
his house had a large stone fireplace
a piano, a garden & orchard.
he collected paintings, mirrors
& walnut furniture.

the father had style
and maybe some gators.
he finessed pesos, pounds & francs
from folks traveling thru town, down
the river, out west or back east. he stayed
serving. awash in wampums. the father was ballin.

his granddaughter, the first non-Native born
in Chicago, was mixed. the first child was mixed.

the father, a product
of terror & rape.
the father, the city
forgets, is mixed

the mix made the British
nervous. a body protestants
couldn't wrap their heads around.

the father is a Black man
pushed out by a white man
rich & thirsty.

DuSable left to die
far from the city
built with his hands.

his mixed hands.
his Black hands.

the father is a Black man.

The Treaty of Chicago
September 26, 1833[1]

Our land has been wasting away ever since the white people became our neighbors,
and we have now hardly enough left to cover the bones of our tribe.
(Potawatomi) Chief Metea

getting the Chiefs to sign
wouldn't be easy. in 1795
the Greenville treaty stole
six miles around the mouth
of the River. city of long cons
fire & fine print. the fight
at Fort Dearborn whites wouldn't
forget, when the Miami tribe
embarrassed the fumbling army
of dumb settlers in fifteen minutes
to take back Roosevelt & Michigan
land simply called earth then.
                    but this'll be the last time
the indigenous dance at the waterway
connecting the Mississippi to the Great Lakes,
a trade post between the Caribbean & New York.
the perfect nexus for whiskey & unbridled capitalism.
this town, such desirable waterfront property
the government will kill to own it.

the pioneers plied Chiefs
all night with bourbon. under intoxication
duress & gun powder, under disease
& white power, in english, an illiterate theft.
they marked the parchment, *X*

Hog Butcher for the World

December 25, 1865²

grid of flesh. source
of labor & meal & mayhem.
cutting edge ingenuity to maim
& murder. a grand dis-assembly
line. innovator of the killing wheel.
steak knife. craver of cattle
earth. neighborhoods gutted. chest
opened by a butcher
                              block
by block.   dissected
like 7th grade science / class.

Chicago is a frog.
Chicago is a pig   fetus

splayed & separated
                                   segregated
from its body
                         politic.
white meat   dark.
an experiment the country watches
                                        & repeats.

town of   viaducts
blvd   motes.
turf wars   & stop signs.
one ways   & circuitous routes.
folks   & people.
          a park
                    in between.
                    a metra train.

          eminent domain.

          the body
quartered.   broken
                              down

                                        somewhere.
a blueprint   picked over
refined.   a carcass
                                city
                        of scraps
                            & sausage.

Albert Parsons Can Hang

November 11, 1887

> *Lay bare the inequities of capitalism; expose the slavery of law; proclaim the tyranny*
> *of government; denounce the greed, cruelty, abominations of the privileged class.*
> **Albert Parsons**[3]

a dumb kid of privilege.
a son of the south.
a descendant of the american revolution.
as a boy, he fought with the confederates.
as a man, he apologized to the Black woman who raised him.
a lover of Lucy,
        part Mestizo & Black radical socialist,
        more dangerous than a thousand rioters.
a typesetter like my grandfather.
a believer in the rights of the worker.
an 8-hour day & 8 to sleep & 8 to play.
a ringer of the alarm.
a white tiger, before Huey, maybe
        dynamite, Jimmie Walker
an organizer in the good times
        summer sunday beer gardens.
a longing for bread or blood.
a leader in the rise of the working class.
a target the barons went after.
an albatross to the merchant prince marshall field.
a defendant in the Haymarket Riot
        no evidence, no fair jury
        railroaded by george pullman.
Albert Parsons
a white man to become
a white man who acted
a white man unbound
        by guilt or other bullshit
a prisoner in cell 29
a writer, live from death row.

How to Be Down

September 18, 1889

Jane Addams from rural Cedarville.
originated in loot & leisure. got shook
the world wasn't like that for all
so she built a table, a house, not perfect
but bout it bout it. her living room big
enough for the whole West Side. kneading
culture as bread & spaghetti eventually
& kindergarten too & garbage pickup
& public parks, a place for immigrants
& a place for Benny Goodman to swing
& Upton Sinclair to report, & W. E. B. Du Bois
to prophesy. a place for Ida B. Wells to debate
& educate Ellen Gates Starr, Florence Kelley
Alice Hamilton, this squad of white women
led by a squat Queer woman. how odd indeed.
how down
                she be.

The L Gets Open

June 6, 1892

the loop would be next.
for now a line, a track
one neighborhood   to another.
magic. transit. a new   street
      different block.   the ethnic lock
         picked
by a steam engine   a camel
           thru the eye
of a needle.
viaduct   crosser. 39th Street
                   to Congress
      31 blocks.
              a working
class
    spaceship   to fly
above
    ground
      & borders.

     all   city
       ours.

The white City
May 1, 1893

the world's fair turned the swamp
utopian lie. classical architecture
a garish nod to old ass empire,
made the poet of steel, Louis Sullivan,
mourn the buildings businessmen
desired to show off. all bluster
& facade. all fronts. the white city
meant to distract, erase the Black
city of smoke & sky, grime & grind.
faces that gutted the land, made it run,
banned, pushed to the side. the face
the city presented to tourists, miles
of magnificence millionaires wanted
out-of-towners to whisper about
on the train trip home. a museum
prison Houdini tried escaping.
fraudulent city of the future built
from scratch, from scraps, hidden
the hands that scraped. beneath
the veneer lurked murder. silent
terror behind white construction.

Eugene Debs Reads Marx in Prison
1895

like Malcolm, memorized the dictionary.

Nature does not produce[4] subjugated
steps. every eve he'd walk the yard
breathing beneath *night's curtain.*
the free sky etched into his head. *on the one side*
owners of money or commodities, on the other men
possessing nothing but their own labour-power
contemplating ways to counter empire.
in *midnight's throne, this relation has no natural basis.*
like the imagination, the heavens spread
common to all historical periods, pages lit
by moon turn. liberated from these walls
he'll walk, waving a new, red banner.

Reversing the Flow of the Chicago River
January 2, 1900

there's shit in the water.
to avoid typhoid fever
an engineering miracle
on par with the pyramids.
canal & quarry men lost
their lives & didn't get credit
or fair compensation. before
it's over Governor Altgeld calls
the national guard to kill some on strike.

                                        but today

Chicago does the impossible.
reverses the flow away
from the great lake michigan
toward the des plaines river
& lockport: this very moment
a man-made nile, a diversion
of millions   of gallons.
by crane & crook
neck, backs breaking rock.
millennia of earth blown with dynamite.
the grit of workers carved a path, bent
the south branch & main stem.
dug 28 miles of canal in the long
purple dusk of a new century.
the sweat & calloused hands
of 8,500 men did the impossible:
shifted the norm
for the health of the young
metropolis. immigrant men
a force, to counter the natural system
so the city   could survive.

The Great Migration
1915–1950

No longer do our lives depend upon the soil, the sun, the rain or the wind; we live by the grace of jobs and the brutal logic of jobs.
Richard Wright, *12 Million Black Voices*

The Defender said come: here
is a promised   land. fill the factories.
the train travels north. leaves at dusk.
leaves the Delta. the train forward
lurches where earth hardens into sky
rises into steel. still Black in the 8 hours
(at least) of chaos. here accents foreign
fast. *a*'s stretch like restrictive covenants
circling Bronzeville. the city builds heaven
for a few. tenements for most. a project
to carve a moment of quiet in the roar
& rumble of machine. lines more rigid
by the minute. lines visible & not;
at the beach, on the train, schools
banks. lines shift, sharpen, root thick.
blueprint into bars: which ones to go
into & not. neighborhoods demarcated
sounds nothing like democracy. separate
& nothing equal. sections. housing
authorities. prisons, windows open
air, industrial, capital, labor under
a different overseer, a different punch
clock. in, off hours, invent in the domestic
space with wares brought from the south
the other side of the atlantic, made electric,
sped up & swinging, Jack Johnson. A. Philip
Randolph will rise from this earth;
a Black mayor, a Black president.

everything will change & nothing will

The Eastland Disaster
July 24, 1915

> *Grim industrial feudalism stands with dripping and red hands behind the whole
> Eastland affair.*
> **Carl Sandburg**

saturday morning, at 6:30 am
western electric workers were ordered
to be on time & dress their best
at the wharf. too poor for holiday
they scrambled in excitement: packed
day bags & made sure dirt disappeared
from their children's faces & fingernails.

the company men would travel to Michigan City
by carriage & the mighty Eastland would carry
secretaries, bean counters, ledger keepers & factory
workers across the great blue body of lake.

the boat'd had problems before.
no one seemed to care. it was
top-heavy like the economy,
the hubris of the city's
over-fed owners.

an hour in, the ship shifted
twenty feet from the shore.
in the middle of the Chicago
river, the boat turned, a whale
of metal flipping on its belly.
hundreds fell from the open
upper deck like drunken pigeons.
hundreds trapped in rooms
beneath, crushed by dead pianos
& falling furniture. mouths stuffed
with gallons of roaring river water

844 people, mostly immigrants
mostly workers died in the Eastland.
my great-grandmother among them.

16

after my grandfather turned
bastard & stalked the north side
with a two-by-four on his shoulder
like the city owed him something
& it did.

The Murder of Eugene Williams

July 27, 1919

the summer was hot as hell.

for relief, his boys brought a raft
to the beach at 25th Street the whole
city's body laid out on water.

lake michigan's powerful current
dragged the raft a few blocks south
a/cross an invisible line in the water.
at 29th Street rocks flew. launched
from white hands on land
they thought theirs alone, to own.
one rocked the temple of Eugene, 17,
off the raft. he drowned in the body
at the bottom of the lake.

& again water graves claim Black
& again white police refuse to arrest
& again white gangs rally

from bridgeport, back of the yards.
white gangs like the hamburgs
like richie daley's crew, like the future
mayors

.

Society for Human Rights
(America's First Gay Rights Organization)
December 10, 1924

at 17, the boy's admitted
into an insane asylum.
institution of electroshock
& hallucinogens, white coats
& sodomy laws. the state
not separated from the church.
they wanted the devil out. he became
double-O seven. shaken & stirred
to action.

Henry Gerber wasn't his name.
a german immigrant boy hiding
in america's skirt. told to meld into
the heteronorm. the boy made illegal.
his fatherland wrote paragraph 175[5]
the bible an arm against him. an outlaw.
an outcast   would go crazy.
          he called a community
together. organized a society
in secret. a space for men to gather
in his home in old town, untouched
by the fear of being found out
& detained & shamed.

John Graves, a Black minister
whose partner was a Pullman porter,
his friend, comrade & confidant signed
the papers to become the first
president of the first organization
in the dumb country, in the young city
45 years before stonewall. Black & White
Chicago men mustered a congregation
                              until they couldn't
until Henry Gerber was fired from his post
office job, arrested, tried three times & lost
his life savings.

he'd go underground, go pseudonym
write newsletter Connection chronicles
from lone apartment bunkers, advocating
for the safety of his being & the being
of those like him & the country being ok
with his being & those like him & the city
country being greater because of it.

Thomas Dorsey, Gospel's Daddy
1932

before the unspeakable
he was Georgia Tom on the road
with Ma Rainey, a raunchy hit maker

seven million records sold.
then his wife Nettie died
in labor. his son two days later.

grief is an unshakeable shelter.
like Coltrane composing *Love
Supreme* in his child's afterglow

Dorsey took to song to mourn
channeled the spirit of rhythm
& blues in juke & segregated joints.

he harnessed the secular
for the sanctified. *Take My Hand,
Precious Lord* the genesis. gospel

called Dorsey's. praise
with piano & tambourine, returning
Black Jesus to the choir, to the ladies

of the church to raise & transform
him, white & stiff on the cross
as he was, into a movement Dr. King

messed with. no one wanted to
publish the songs he sang. so
he made his own label: House

of Music; independent, divine. self
-determined. tryin to run the devil
out; white, blue-eyed or otherwise.

Gwendolyn Brooks Stands in the Mecca
1936

I wrote about what I saw and heard in the street. There was my material.
Gwendolyn Brooks

she slang snake oils
at 19. her small hands
moving love potions
out bottles for some kind
of doctor. stalking halls
listening to the masses
stuffed in kitchenettes.
blocks of brick. floors
of Black lives. every
day people fighting
& fucking & struggling
to make it. sometimes
they didn't. nose ripe
with onion fumes
rising like the people's
will in the warpland.
she took rich snapshots
of the poor. some rhythm
rattling around her head.
each sound an ornament:
a key turning the tumbler,
faucets praising the body
with lukewarm water,
the laughter of kids
& criminals. the lost
girls. she kept count
of them, each syllable
stuck in a handbag
in her head, waiting
til she got home
to lay every precious
note on the table
right in front of her
nose, the tiny gems
she'd gather thru

the day, all
the ingredients
she'd need to sit
& begin to write
a new literature,
a new world.

Hansberry vs. Lee
November 12, 1940

american racism helped kill him
Lorraine Hansberry

her father knew a good deal
when he saw it. a real estate
man building a Black belt
in Bronzeville growing
like a belly spilling into Woodlawn.
the whites got to clutching their pearls.
built picket fences taller, whiter. guarded
them with ordinances nobody voted for
& bombs that burst in Black homes freely
as the 4th of July.
                        Carl stayed strapped
with lawyers, reading endless court documents
in the wee hours under dimming light
& the coming dawn. Du Bois & Robeson
ate in the kitchen when they were in town
encouraging him to fight & bust the barriers down
all the way up   to the supreme court
                                        he went.

& little Lorraine,
ten years old at betsy ross
elementary, listened in the corner
with Langston in her lap,
taking notes the whole
time, writing down her father's face
how it sagged, sad, what he said.
his wrestling & anguish. her diary
became the first Black woman
on broadway, the great white way.
the story of her daddy's fight, how even
victory is death for Black men
in america.

Muddy Waters Goes Electric
1945

bars & rent parties roar. motherfuckers won't shut up.
the acoustic guitar's an impotent whimper in the throat
of war machines. some country shit won't cut it.
Muddy slick, like his hair, like the puddles & creeks
he played in, in Clarksdale.   a long way

from sharecropping & his dead mama.
he drives a truck delivering venetian blinds & works
a paper mill making lumber lay like linen.

Uncle Joe got him an ax with fangs. he plugged in
& shook fire out. the amp spit licks that wrapped
around necks of macks talkin weak game & zip.
fuck a pick, it remind him too much of Mississippi.
pluck this metal with hands that worked the earth,
that call folk home & throw them thru the future
out a plate glass window. he a conjured a time
machine.
                    (white boys tried to it pick up
but couldn't access its Black magic. clapton,
a poor mimic. the stones, a colonial bore.)

McKinley Morganfield sits up on a stool
around 43rd Street & shoots lightning out
his fingers, a jolt thru the city. he makes
the blues jump. he shocks the world.

Nelson Algren Meets Simone de Beauvoir at the Palmer House
February 21, 1947

beneath ornate ceilings, in the grand room
on plush cushions, they drank martinis
he couldn't stomach & she didn't understand
a word he said. he thought she looked
like a french school teacher, a good-lookin one
who in a few days he'd read about in
the new yorker. he's a different sort, she thought.
not like the men she'd tolerate in the parisian cafe society,
high-minded intellectuals who'd rather talk than lust.

she returned in april. he took her
to the polish bars in wicker park,
to his apartment without a bathroom,
garbage piling in the alleys. he'd show
her a jail, the electric chair, men strung
on heroin. a city/country taking it
on the chin. he had a chip
on his shoulder, a second city complex.

she's a modern wave french Feminist.
the loved, lauded, chic Queen of the existentialists.

he's a Chicago artist cursed in the middle, unappreciated
in a moment McCarthy will try to ban his realism & wit.

she loved his grit, the precision of craft
honed thru years of devotion. the gift
of pen & more. he made her come
to his city again & for the first time.

they were destined
to nose dive. be out
of reach. an impossible
bird & bear bound
to the cities that made them.

Algren died without anyone
claiming his body. his heart
attacking minutes after
a reporter asked of her.

de Beauvoir was buried
alongside Sartre in Paris
but bore Algren's silver
ring on her bone, forever.

Pickle with a Peppermint Stick
white flight after World War II, 1948–1978

*Integration is the period between the arrival of the first Black and the departure of
the last white.*
   Saul Alinsky

             is some
       Maxwell Street hold over.
        brine, tangy. crisp since 1898
      when the first wave of immigrant
      jews slid safe from europe & made
      shtetls. schmattas tied over the wide
      hips of Bubbes preparing vegetables
      for the hawk & long winter ahead. a
      pickle's perfect for lunch, some snack
      out a jar: garlic, peppercorn & dill.
      enterprise young hustler. henry ford
      off the block. out the hood. innovate.
      dream america in the trunk & church
      of the dollar. amass. mass produce in
      plastic. produce plastic. exit the shtetl
     for the shrubs of the suburbs. leave relics
      in the corner store. leave poor, darker new
     immigrants behind in the corner store. leave
    something for them to suck on. the South Side
    became the new north, became the old south.
      Harriet's railroad stopped too soon. shtetls
     grew ghettos. Blacks from the south, stopped
      on the stoop, but the stoop already claimed.
       the corner already owned by someone else.
      Jim Crow lives here too. the sour too much
      to take after coming all that way. the north
       promised roads of gold & bellies of milk.
      salt & vinegar too much bitter to swallow.
       too much history to inherit & repeat.
       the peppermint stick is some sweet/ness
        to help america go down. some castor
         oil & BBQ. some addition & innovation
        kids with hot tongues playing with fire
       demanded for fun, a change of pace &
        palate they shanked the pickle with
        a peppermint stick like a vd exam.
        something here is sick & burning.
          here's some cool to extinguish
            the fire, some mint to ease
               all this funk.

Sun Ra Becomes a Synthesizer
October 20, 1952

> *I'm not a minister, I'm not a philosopher, I'm not a politician, I'm in another category.*
> -Sun Ra

thecollegedropoutconscientiousobjector
EgyptologistBlackfuturistGarveyiteoccultist
interplanetarytranshistoricalorator. at night
he played bump & grind in Cal City strip clubs
but in the small apartment in Washington Park
he learned to synthesize: Themi research, race
etymologist fusing ideas & tone in dissonance
& modality. minor, major sound effects to swing
to rocket fly towards an Afro-Future. wheeling
mimeographed dissertations on 55th Street
politicking with Black Muslims & Hebrew Israelites
in a gold Pharaoh nemes headdress & glitter cape.
today he shed his slave name & Herman Blount
became Sun Ra, a vessel taking trips to Saturn
way before any white man made it to the moon.

hugh hefner, a Play Boy

December 1953

> *A woman reading* Playboy *feels a little like a Jew reading a Nazi manual.*
> **Gloria Steinem**

his first wife Mildred cheated. her guilt
assuaged. she allowed him to play, boy.

they split. he boasted of the twelve cover girls
in a subscription cycle, he'd bed eleven. never pay, boy.

captain of industry & sexual harassment, selling
the dream. a new hi-fi. just press play, boy.

the parties, a wink, a club house, cosby friend
offering quaaludes, *thigh openers.* he preyed, boy.

flaccid maleness. plastic surgery, eurocentric
ageless, airbrushed. his fantasy, a play. boy

with a mansion. potato chips & porn. knockoff
chic, convinced he's a bon vivant, a playboy.

skin stretched, ascot knot over his gizzard. silk pajama sleaze.
when he realize G-d's feminine, he'll wish he woulda prayed, boy.

the walt disney of misogyny, mainstreaming objectification. bunnies
splayed bare, just supposed to lay there, silent, in playboy.

Mamie Till Bears the Movement

Roberts Temple Church of G-d, 4021 S. State St.
September 3, 1955

I wanted the world to see what they did to my baby.
Mamie Till-Mobley

Mamie told 'em keep the casket open.
Mamie told 'em keep the casket open.
Mamie told 'em keep the casket open.
Mamie told 'em keep the casket open.
Mamie told 'em keep the casket open.
Mamie told 'em keep the casket open.
Mamie told 'em keep the casket open.
Mamie told 'em keep the casket open.
Mamie told 'em keep the casket open.
Mamie told 'em keep the casket open.
Mamie told 'em keep the casket open.
Mamie told 'em keep the casket open.
Mamie told 'em keep the casket open.
Mamie told 'em keep the casket open.

king daley Unfurls His burnham Plan
1958–1965

daley's plan took
105 acres in one fell swoop.
closed the entry point to immigrants
from everywhere. one of the only
integrated neighborhoods,
old Maxwell Street.

the wives of city workers organized
protests. jammed their aged, round
bodies into his fifth floor city hall office
to throw books & foreign expletives
at the mayor who sighed & turned
a dumb, dead ear & corned-beef heart.

UIC is built in the architectural style of brutalism.
what was said to be a bridge to the community
was a concrete casket. a cement balloon
expanding on inflated budgets & the mayor's hot air
a big bad wolf blowing houses down. eight thousand
people displaced. six hundred businesses.
the campus a typhoon on the near west side.
university hall a grave marker, a castle
in the heavens. the administration looks down
like the peregrine falcons who made refuge
on the 28th floor: birds of a feather, predators of the sky.

The Division Street Riots

June 12, 1966

the summer of the first
Puerto Rican Day parade, the hood
bomba-d in the face of imperialists.
cops felt some type of way. chased
Aracelis Cruz thru alleys & shot him
in the back. neighbors stepped
off porches, from in front of coolers
to assist the young man laying
on the ground in the lot near Damen
& the police protected the land
grab with batons & brute force & beat
abuelitas armed with only chancletas.

for 2 days, Division became the Island
unified. the sun rose & soon the metal
flags. the iron of Oscar Lopez. Humboldt
Park to La Clark, Puerto Ricans aligned
across redlines with Panthers, a coalition
of Brown & Black, the bosses' greatest fear.
Division Street became a gauntlet
a proving ground. Cha Cha Jimenez[6]
would feel the earth quiver & kneel
before its majesty, in isolation, in county
throwing up junk & sins & the Young
Lords will rise like the sun
& daughters & sons will defend
abuelitas armed with chancletas
in the name of the island & ancient
G-ds, in solidarity & self-determination.

the fight, the stand
the stake in the land

from here, a people
will not move.

Martin Luther King Prays in Marquette Park

August 5, 1966

> *That is no Jerusalem on Lake Michigan.*
> **MLK**

he journeyed to the hot
cauldron of the South Side
to pry apartments open. make them
livable, not slumlord roach traps.
his people here told him not to.
Jesse & nem warned these white clans
weren't a dumb collection of farm hands.
the whole city's a white gang.

but King couldn't listen with all the blood in his ear.

in the month the poor & old
wilt cuz the city whites & boils
bricks, sticks & epithets flew.
one rocked King in the crown.
brought him to his knees. made
his blood faucet & mix with dirt
white men stole & misspelled.

what curse did he utter
beneath his breath, onto the land
we reek of & revel in.
what prayer did he plant.
what whisper raised
a forest, a Chairman Fred.

what mark of Cain did he cut
into the park named for french colonists
into the city of no peace. his blood
a potion that parted a sea to lead whites
to the land promised in schaumburg
a sham burg, a death. a dead; see
america in parts. a King bent
beneath the furnace mouth
of a white mass, an american
church, a dragon he couldn't slay.

Studs Terkel Drops a Mixtape
January 16, 1967[7]

it started in the lobby of his parents'
boarding house; a thousand colloquialisms
& idiosyncratic speech patterns. it started
with a kid in a cab, the discipline
of empathy. the tape recorder
a time machine. a teleporter. mirror
& mountaintop. it started talking
to 200 everyday people. no celebrity.
edited 70. ages 15 to 90: bar owners & alcoholics,
a Native American boiler man, activists,
racists, teachers & the forgotten who live
alone in furnished rooms. populism
on the page. guerilla journalism
before it was called that. it started
in Bug House Square: the denizen forum
for radicals & miscreants, the genius & insane
lines blurred, irrelevant. here is the collected
memory of a city that is the country
the microcosm. the division in us all.

Carl Sandburg Village (Where My Parents Met)
1967–1969

When we did Sandburg, the other streets around it were full of flophouses. So Sandburg Village was like a military operation. We had to have the sufficient size and numbers to go in there and push the enemy back. Coldly. Like D-Day.
john cordwell, chief architect of Carl Sandburg Village

the apartments were new & beautiful & appeared out of nowhere. my moms parents worried she moved so close to Cabrini, so close, to so many Black people. she left junior college, got a job selling downtown at a department store. she moved in with her friend Helain. flocks of young white people came to the new Sandburg Village, built as a buffer between the wealthy center, a growing Puerto Rican neighborhood to the north & high-rise projects housing Black lives like a prison to the east. the management so paranoid & adamant in their protection of the downtown hold, they put the national guard on top of the roof during the rebellion after Martin King was murdered. the onslaught they feared, never came.

there was a pool on the roof, an alluring feature. my father gigged there as a lifeguard. it was his third. one at a bar, one at a school. he lived close with his buddy Gary, in a coach house at 1338 North LaSalle. he moved from Edgewater south to be near the gigs & a growing scene of college grads beginning to nightlife on Division Street. what were these young whites called then: intruders, pioneers, pawns. in struts my mother, one afternoon, my father on duty. he asked to see her key, her membership for admission. she was not having it that day or any in her life & promptly gave him the finger, the middle, with the quickness. she complained in tones unnecessary for a saturday at 2. my father listened, nodded, waited til she finished, then, unmoved, still asked to see her key. she chucked them at the table. the keys hopped into his hand like a shortstop. my pops was impressed, surprised by the flex. she walked away before he could say anything. he saw her pass, in all her glory, and his weak, lone response was: *damn.*

after cooling off in the chlorine she apologized by flirting. invited him & Gary for dinner that night. they cooked & ate & talked about people they might have in common, the convention, the riots, all the change the city/country was mired in. my father worked at a bar called the Store, not far on Clark Street. Helain & my moms went. he poured drinks. she watusied. they caught each other's eye & moms mouthed the words *i love you.* she

was wild like that, reckless cause she had nothing. my father looked behind, around, shocked, put a finger to his chest, mouthed a question back:
me. she nodded & kept dancing.

she stayed on a stool, an elbow, & waited for him. they went back to her
place, in the Sandburg Village & they each swear all they did was talk
night, into the new day, witnessing the morning in her new apartment, getting to know one another in the new city/country, changing by fist & fire.

Wall of Respect
August 27, 1967

> *white people can't stand / the wall...Black beauty hurts them—*
> **Haki Madhubuti, *The Wall***

picasso ain't got shit on us[8]

so said the nine who portrait-ed:
Malcolm & Muhammad,
Nina & Bird, Marcus & Amiri
at 43rd & Langley.

a few weeks after
the bird/woman sculpture
revealed politicians don't know
much bout anything, 'specially art.
on the side of a tavern
next to Johnny's tv & radio repair
a store that fixes the image, the wall
a shrine to Black creativity.

a 24-hour gallery where little girls
could see women who looked
like their mother. the people
came, *a Black stampede.*[9] a gathering
spot, an outdoor museum, no entrance
fee, free. a Black festival of chromatics
body & hue.   from here
street art & public mural
movements. walls & spray cans
will sprout, a people's art.
the city, a canvas.

AfriCOBRA
1968

African Commune of Bad Relevant Artists.
bad the way Run-DMC defines it. a crew
trying to transcend the *i* for *WE*, Muhammad Ali.
relevant like how most art ain't cuz institutions
beholden to the loaned collections of the rich
& they don't want a painting holding a knife
to their neck.

Jeff Donaldson, Wadsworth Jarrell, Gerald Williams,
& Barbara Jones-Hogu made Kool-Aid colors for superReal
people. colors the people would be drawn to: the luster
of a just-washed head, the glint of sunglasses, grandparents'
shea-butter sheen, Afro puffs & a girl in a yellow overcoat.

after them: Kerry James Marshall, SLANG
Krista Franklin, Hebru Brantley, Amanda Williams,
art that hasn't been made, prints created
so an 8-year-old in Woodlawn or L-Town
may wake every morning & see themselves.

45

The Assassination of Chairman Fred Hampton

December 4, 1969

the Panthers came home to the West Side
near Chicago Stadium where the bulls play
& no memorial sits. a statue for mike
but nothing for Mark Clark & Chairman Fred.

what shook hoover: Black children eating
breakfast, starting the day with sustenance
& the free conversation between the real rainbow
coalition: Young Lords & Young Patriots,
the non-aggression pact the Panthers negotiated
an alliance of street organizations that loved
the second amendment a lot & Black people
the most.

secobarbital, a sedative, was slipped in his drink
by an informant. Fred to sleep forever in the blood bed
next to Akua, 8 months blooming. at 4:45am cpd & fbi
bust thru the door, knew exactly where the Chairman
was cuz the blueprint, cointelpro. 2 shots point blank
into the mind of a genius. Fred of Maywood, 21 years
old, executed by the state for being with the proletariat
against the pigs. the last words on his lips:

i am a revolutionary

Don L. Lee Becomes Haki Madhubuti

1972

lee was not a revolutionary name:
an ill fit after the army he served
& left, after his mother's decline & death,
after reading Richard Wright & seeing his
body in Black   for the first time.

Haki was given by a committee of ancestors.
a reclamation & renaming. they allowed him
to reintroduce himself: Haki means justice.
Madhubuti is four syllables, means precise.
means dependable. what other poet/writer
teacher been more dependable in the struggle
for justice.

Haki Madhubuti means long haul & fire, means
the work for real, means storefronts will blossom
to Black institutions, means build with Black stones
means anybody down to build, means by any, reinvention
of the world, the word to burn. lee an effigy to the white
wor(l)d left behind   smoldering & ashy.

Haki Madhubuti means the Black future ahead.

The Chicago 21 Plan
September 1973

I'll tell you what's wrong with the Loop. . . . It is one word: B-L-A-C-K.
arthur rubloff, real estate developer, in the *Chicago Daily News*

oak and chandelier. opaque light
filtering thru the day's death. an ash
tray near each fat white hand.
the original canopy of cigar smoke.
what is meant by back room dealing.

a plan to centralize in the loop.
to build a mote, a fortress. a gold
coast. gold mine. mine. take dead
tracks & build condos. river norths.
south loops to stave off white flight.
to usher white folk into condos.
into printers row. choke Cabrini
of its green.

pay to play. pay to stay. everyone was in
on the act. the universities & big businesses.
hold the center. transform blues to white
collar. daley to daley. Black to white. flight
from the past. erasure by another name:
gentrification's birth certificate.

Leaving Aldine
1978

my pops wanted to make his own
name. build a restaurant with his on it.
my brother was not yet. i was & remember
the movers. the men who worked & drove
a truck as i would. there was not a lot left
in the apartment. soon there would not be
my pops in the house.
                  but before
at the window, i was
playing with the blinds. spider
man on the television not yet
repossessed. the bead chain
my web. my earliest memory
the apartment, the city. a hope
something would make me   stick

Ode to Steppin
1978

when you could only buy 78s
& the jitterbug slowed to smooth.
when the lindy hop landed
in a little bit of bread & the hawk
adorned the body in long coats
& fox furs. when gents were majestic
& ladies mirrored the men, one foot
at a time, but did it backwards
meaning they went harder
but you couldn't tell cuz the glide
& off time cool was no sweat at all.
when Jeffree Perry should've been
a star & Black Mary was Chicago's Queen,
stepper sets filled Bronzeville ballrooms
& basements & weekend banquet halls.
when people's parents still married
or at least together cuz of the kids.
when you could raise a family in the city
E&J away a weekend with a woman
in one hand & a handkerchief in the other.
when you were a gouster or ivy league.
when high or low end wasn't a death sentence.
when the middle class was an aspiration
the city/country seemed to believe
& folks could take some time to get there
at least til Monday or at least til Sunday
morning when the lights would come on
like the sun at the lake no one could afford
to live near. when the weekend was over
but *love's gonna last* like the stubborn couple
at the end of the night, when the DJ's gone
quiet & the chairs overturn on tables
& the turntables tumbleweed
but the 4/4 still ghost-steps
in their bodies at the end of the dance
floor, quiet as they float above
portable wood tiles or taut linoleum
as one. when one night is all
anyone ever needs.

Disco Demolition

July 12, 1979

White males . . . see disco as the product of homosexuals, blacks, and Latins, and
therefore they're the most likely to respond to appeals to wipe out such threats to their
security.
   Dave Marsh, Rolling Stone

steve dahl donned a helmet
a military uniform, drove the diamond
in an army jeep. dahl was a white
middle brow disc jock. his listeners
white men in the middle of america.
factories were packing up. the world
promised began to look other/wise.

dahl & white sox management
made a promo night to attract
a dwindling fan base
in a subpar season.
it was 98 cents to get in
if fans brought a record
to be blown up in center field.

            Disco was dance
            for the generation after Vietnam.
            sped up Soul dreamt in Gay
            clubs, Black & Latino & more.
            & the whites came
            & the whites came.

tonight they came, aroused
with beer & records to burn.
a vinyl bonfire. Black records
aflame.

            comiskey park
            in bridgeport, home of the dick
            daleys. they fell in love with their mother's
            corned beef & cabbage & an architectural
            appreciation for viaducts.

white men hopped turnstiles, ticket lines.
more bodies crammed in comiskey
than there'd ever been. Chicago was playing
Detroit. cities dwindling like the white majority.

dahl set the fire. a ringmaster,
a comic imp, a cowardly warlord.
a small pop & boom! fans
stormed the field, littered
the grass with bottles & concession debris.
records sliced the air like weapons.
long hairs in lee jeans & cut-off
t-shirts slid into second. they stole home
again. a crater burned into center
field. a white mob on the diamond.
the game postponed, forfeit, rigged
from the beginning. Harry Caray couldn't
control the crowd or get them back
in their seats. the police were called:
uncles & fathers came to chase
their sons. the force restrained.
no one was shot or beat to death.
there were scoldings, few arrests.
steve dahl walked free.

> Chicago
> would grind disco in a steel mill
> run it thru electric sockets til it bumped
> grimy. til it was House & jacked
> the body. til the technology
> displaced white disc jocks.
> made them obsolete, old machines
> dancing in their graves.

mayor byrne Moves Into & Out of Cabrini Green
Easter Sunday, April 19, 1981

the first night
the mayor & her husband
watched the academy awards,
april fools in a two-bedroom
apartment furnished
by montgomery ward
in the most infamous
project on the planet
protected by 2 bodyguards
6 squad cars. her publicist
said she'd return to her gold
coast apartment a few blocks
east for a change
of clothes or perhaps a week
end, tho residents saw her sneak
in every morning & out each night
                    for three weeks   she lasted.

& such is whiteness

the ability to de-robe
a life/style & return to privilege
awash in skin, adorned in birth
rite. a retreat, a return
back across heavily patrolled
borders of wealth
& white / working & not   white.

on easter the mayor's blonde
ambition presides over an egg
hunt, the residents picket,
chant: *we need jobs, not eggs*
jane byrne is the ku klux klan

the mayor as invader
conquistador, missionary:
idyllic words backed by force.

on the day Jesus returns
the mayor flees.

Ron Hardy Plays the Record Backwards
The Music Box. 1982–1987

I can imagine him praying before he put on his turntables.
Adonis, Chicago acid house pioneer

Robert Williams gave him the run of the place.
a playground of speakers. an open studio to mad
scientist. shirt open, he'd dr. frankenstein sound.
stitch Black soul to new wave. one afternoon
high as shit, he must've flipped. turned the needle
upside down, spun the tone arm over, propped the wax
on a cylinder to keep it spinning, pushed the platter
to earth & played it backwards. on beat. his mind
forever changed. on heroin, the music slowed to a nod.
he sped it up. dancers jacked new velocities. sent
a generation to their parents' record collections
to rescue history. to dig & cut it up. resuscitate it
for the people to feel in a way that could move them
to (a)movement. break & pose & vogue before madonna
stole. before it was called that. from Chatham, a whole
city seeking sanctuary on his dance floor to get loose
& live & high, to find themselves aligned.
a fix, of chaos, in order to get free.

The Assassination of Rudy Lozano
June 8, 1983

a man driven by a search for unity among people
Harold Washington on Rudy Lozano

he was kicked out of high school
looking for Latino history. his curiosity
built Juarez, rivers at Cermak & Ashland.
Pilsen, his home. Harold, his homie
he helped elect thru organizing
the neighborhood & Del Rey tortilla
workers. mustache like a push broom.
a texas Chicano, Chicago son
whose sister & sons fight sin
fronteras. the city
so shook, it armed itself.
sent a 17-year-old
into the summer night
into the Lozano kitchen
with a hammer trembling
before the scariest architectural
idea: a bridge built between
Black & Brown workers, a class
alliance, a border crossing.

Marc Smith Invents the Poetry Slam
1984

the city's a racket
so loud you can't hear yourself shit.
space for quiet some yuppie luxury.

Marc built homes with his hands.
moved metal, lunch pail, hot thermos
to a saloon. in the evening stories came.

the apple fell on his head
after work at 1758 North Honore
the Get Me High Lounge:
red lamps, music ledgers
lining the john, smoke
& flannel everywhere:

america loves sport
but needs story.

he handed scorecards to the regulars.
Tony Fitzpatrick, the referee.
Patricia Smith, the city's empress.

Marc stood on top of a table
in his father's coat & pulled a poem
from night. part Sandburg
part Saul Alinsky, for a few seconds
the din sunk to the floor. even the drunks
listened, remembered their own
mother, their bum day, an outrage.

the poem no longer untouched
in a museum. it paraded the streets
on the shoulders of giants & pigeons.
it sat in a church hat on the bus
& wound its way into the throats
of every man, woman & non-binary
being.

as he spoke the last word,
a locomotive rumbling
into the station, gasping
screeching, letting the steam
out, he extended his hand
& ear to hear all the words:
& he pulled the next one up
& the next one
& the next

Collateral Damage
1985

coke was cheap & stacked
on tables, hidden in cute purses
in glass vials. around at lunch time
at the merchandise mart
where moms moved lines
for big stores carrying the latest fashion.

                   i don't think she's
who the CIA envisioned as clientele.

she's young & single & struggling
to make rent. she'd hit Faces,
the disco on rush street & come home high
& not make rent. & we'd move again.
the suburbs our diaspora:
the divorce took us from Sanders Road.
there was the ranch house on Walters.
the townhome in Pheasant Creek.
the one near mama.
the one behind the Phillips '76.
the one behind white hen.

                   i'm forgetting a few.

white had a hold of my family
too. my home, a chess piece,
a chair holding a parking spot
in the snow, a vacated split
level. an eviction, notice: white
working. we lived in cooked
county.

The Day Harold Died
November 27, 1987

we went to the rock & roll mcdonald's the wednesday before thanks-
giving. moms took a half-day. she was fly & a fashion rep—high on a
mound of white. i was 12 & lived with Harold for four years. he was
somewhere between Malcolm X & Martin King & a Black grandfather
whose feet i wanted to sit at. he was barack before barack; a Chicago
hope, a Chicago King who brought Latins & Blacks together like Frank-
ie Knuckles. the first Black mayor in the city of DuSable.

the rock & roll mcdonald's was filled with sequined capes, shiny 50s bar
stools, elvis/beatles posters in half a hall of fame of white-washed mem-
orabilia. not a Buddy Guy pic in sight, not a Howling Wolf guitar lick on
the jukebox. in the city of Muddy Waters the golden arches were a white
heaven where jump blues turned vanilla shake.

i knew i didn't like white music & was beginning to know the extent
white people lied on history & in the parking lot that day i knew a lunch
out with moms & my brother was a luxury. i knew this was how rich
people must live, ordering, off menus. i knew at any time things could be
taken away; electricity, fathers, mothers in handcuffs.

we ate in the car. moms juggling a fleeting to-do list in her brain. my
brother, a boy monk in the front seat trying to visualize some future
stability. his heart still, a soft fruit, sweet. he carried toys in his pocket,
wanted a transformer for Hanukkah, hoped that what we were, was not
the limit of what we could become.

the car was on cuz the hawk[10] was swooping between buildings on On-
tario & Ohio like a flood & the radio was audible & murmuring, tuned to
WBBM or WGN or maybe even GCI if moms let us have a say that day,
for once in our life. we were mid-bite in the damp & growing cold of november & the radio whispered, Harold was dead. it was the afternoon &
i didn't think someone could leave with the sun still out, a giant shining
overhead like some Moses, some Tubman, promising a possible land. the
radio said he sipped his coffee, slumped at his table, his heart attacked &
he was gone.

i thought we'd have to move next, like when the landlord says go.
The Mayor was gone & soon too, the people.

Patronage

February 29, 1992

If I can't help my sons then they can kiss my ass! I make no apologies to anyone. There are many men in this room whose fathers helped them and they went on to become fine public servants. If a man can't put his arms around his sons and help them, then what's the world coming to?
    richard m. daley, January 2, 1977

a city of stupid sons. boys being
boys. stealing their father's new white
chevy blazer & driving an hour & a half
around the U of the lake to their summer home
in michigan to get turnt & let off catholic boy
steam & drink, pull out a shotgun, a baseball bat
& beat an indiana boy's brain to blood clot.

no daley will serve
time. time is for other sons
without birthright. without a firm
that will receive millions in sewage
contracts, shit money filling up
bank accounts or the internet
contract for o'hare or the tur global
investment firm where daley & his boy
sell off Chicago's public goods
to the highest bidder. bitter
men & their dumb sons.

daley's daddy made his son
the state's attorney despite failing
the bar twice & never trying
a case. when evidence of police torture
graced his desk in the early '80s
it was ignored. his ignorance made him
mayor.
        & what
        father wouldn't
want to stand for his son.
make a call or tell a judge
over lunch at the Chicago club

64

to take it easy, let the family
handle it.
                    patronage
is a Chicago word for family
for taking care of one's own
& what father would disagree
or wouldn't want to spare his son
from jail or death, a desire for a life
easier.than his own.

Fresh to Death

Summer 1992

In Chicago, police created a whole new crime category, Starter Jacket Murders
Jet Magazine, May 11, 1992

starter jackets were the coldest
second skin. they'd glitter
in the wholesale windows
of Maxwell Street storefronts
like flags or primary-colored
emeralds. shone from Black
poets on Yo! MTV Raps.
Chicago, Hornets, mascots, cities
emblazoned on the chest
like tribal tats, religions, gang
affiliations. clean sport cuffs
& collar. snap buttons & sheen.
the coolest wore them open even
in the crisp air, airing rope gold
& white tees. a coat perfect
for the fall. so much loot, you'd
get slapped just for thinkin
bout askin your mama for one.
oil-slick arms just outta reach
like everything in america.
so cold it seemed reasonable
this could be the ocean of satin
somebody might die over.

Molemen Beat Tapes
1993

were copped from Gramaphone.
cassettes jammed into the factory
issued stereo deck of the hoopty
i rolled around in. a bucket. bass
& drum looped with some string
sample, fixed. a sliver of perfect
adjusted. the scrapes of something
reconstituted. there was so much
space to fill. an invitation to utter.
Iqra- Allah said to the prophet
Muhammad (peace be upon Him).
a to b-side & around again. a circle
a cipher. i'd drive down & back
in my moms dodge for the latest
volumes of sound. i'd stutter
& stop & begin again. lonesome
& on fire. none. no one i knew
rapped. i'd recite alone on Clark Street
free, styling, shaping, my voice
a sapling, hatchling, rapping
my life, emerging in the dark
of an empty car.

  ✶

there was a time when hip-hop felt like a secret
society of wizards & wordsmiths. magicians
meant to find you or you were meant to find
like rappers i listened to & memorized in history
class talked specifically to me, for me.

  ✶

& sometimes
you'd see a kid whisper to himself
in the corner of a bus seat & you
asked if he rhymed & traded a poem

a verse like a fur pelt / trapping.
some gold or food. this sustenance.

you didn't have to ride solo anymore.

*

Jonathan was the first kid i met who rapped. he was Black
from a prep school, wore ski goggles on top his head & listened
to Wu-Tang which meant he was always rhyming about science
& chess. his pops made him read Sun Tzu. his mans was Omega
a fat Puerto Rican who wrote graffiti & smoked bidis.

& they'd have friends
& the back seat would swell
& the word got passed / scooped like a ball
on the playground. you'd juggle however long
your mind could double-dutch. sometimes you'd take
what you were given / lift off like a trampoline
rocket launch. sometimes you'd trip & scrape
your knees. tongue-tied, not quick. words stuck
on loop, like like words, stuck, like that. but break
thru, mind, knife sharp, mind darts
polished & gleaming we'd ride
for the sake of rhyming. take the long way
home or wherever the fuck we were going
cruise down Lake Shore & back, blasting
blazing. polishing these gems.
trying to get our mind right.

Graffiti Blasters: An Erasure (A Buff)
1993[11]

Graffiti   scars   hurt

        Chicago
    blast   trucks
    use baking soda   high
    pressure   remove
    stone   mineral.
a model
    for other cities foreign
    WarsawPragueMilanChina   Arizona
the City's anti-crime   program
         depends
         on removal   we make every effort
         to remove.

The Department works very closely   with Police   will apprehend
vandals
               deface.

No Chicago   has to tolerate   graffiti.
Please join us   in eliminating   a beautiful city

The Violent Crime Control
& Law Enforcement Act

September 13, 1994

made the streets gaunt
ghost like. gave daley
the impetus to cut heads
of gangs with abandon
& no oversight. 100,000
new police. 9.7 billion for
mass incarceration. inmate
education no more
Malcolms or Etheridges.
jail rigid, more separatist.
more private stock
options on how to pile
minors. magicians
making students
vanish, school to prison
pipeline, urban out
fitted, since this bill
clinton passed & rahm
rammed thru congress
making democrats
republican. when the country
tricked the huddled masses
the poor & tired deported
kids kidnapped off the block.
there's a 33 percent chance
each Black man will be
in chains again. 3 strikes
means life. means gone
til november like the jobs.
means the 13th amendment
applies here, means you can't
apply here. jobs obsolete.
delete. means you'll be
deleted. defeated. the city
creates an indentured
servitude, a new service
sector. a new slavery.

The Etymology of Chicago Joe
September 27, 1994

> *Slim was fresh, Joe*
> **Common, "I used to love H.E.R"**

in Chicago, we call men *Joe*

       from the hebrew, *Yosef*
Jacob's eleventh son. Jesus's stepdad.
as in Louis, Frazier, DiMaggio.

as in cup of. *Joe Blow*
an average fellow. a generic man.
G.I. with the kung-fu grip
though most *Joes* have trouble
holding a grip. the every man
Algren wrote of, *Joe Felso*
the hustler & hustled.
shoeless & misunderstood
despite hall of fame numbers.

Joe is always looking for work.
Joe is always looking over his shoulder.
Joe gets nervous when someone walks up on him too quick.
Joe gets nervous when cops around.
Joe is illegal.
Joe is an immigrant.
Joe is a regular guy trying to make it
& for that you can get knocked
on the head or worse
in this city. the grind keeps
Joe's nose to the stone
streets paved in potholes.

Joe should have his number retired.
Joe is a retired numbers runner.

too many *Joes* have county-issued numbers.
too many *Joes* numb & unaccounted for.

Joe, a sure thing you can count on
Joe is tired of running.

P. BRANTON

72

Common's Resurrection
October 25, 1994

beloved, know how amped we was:
the first time the culture rooted
in Chicago stories & slang. locales
our own, on the bus to touch home. here
the names of streets we knew, ran. a young
man we'd seen off Cottage, at the jam, heard
on WHPK. he sounded like the city
we loved that will never love us back.
sounded cold, like he had one. on wax
for the whole country to hear. an international
megaphone a dozen years after The Message
loud & clear: the children of Gwendolyn Brooks
are rappers. his pops played ABA ball.
moms, a doctor of education. a Chicago son
speaking what he/we knew: Andre Hatchett,
carfare, jewtown. Stony Isle, DJ Pharris, Leon's
BBQ. high schools we went to, fought with
played against, girls we hollered at. the greatest
extended metaphor hip-hop ever wrote.
monuments for what was/is here. *when
mad was tall & phat was cold.* we loved
Twista who rapped so quick we needed
a translator. DA Smart, Fast Eddie
the super bowl shuffle, a slew of graffiti
writers who went to war with mayor daley
but Common put Chicago at the intersection
of the culture, made Ice Cube an actor. mike
on vinyl, a ring you could hear in the sweetgums
& sycamores. footprints in the sand at lake
shore, a blueprint for the many to come.

The Supreme Court Makes Color Illegal
March 3, 1995

Residents of Chicago will be the losers, for they forfeit the benefits of spray paint.
Justice John Paul Stevens

nothing vivid, nothing out
              the ordinary, nothing off
grey   scale. out   the lines
of black & white.   (whites only)
             nothing
                cops can't read
       think is a gang
every kid
       of color with color
a gang. gang, what
             is a crew
a community, policed.
even the art, the innovation
gone. brush, color gone.
         a country
of bone & art school.
       everything here illegal:
art, people of color   with color
       nothing with color
nothing that questions
            that jars the mind
       aware awake.   a wake
only. no spray
paint. bullets ok.
grave markers ok.
targets ok
the store, on backs
of bodies of color with color ok.
       ok   color, the problem.
       color the criminal.
criminalize color, ok. ok.

Erasing the Green
September 27, 1995[12]

tearin down the ' jects creatin plush homes
Common, "Resurrection"

towers torn before 9-11.
gaping wounds. living
rooms gut bare. painted
walls for the city to see
brick tumble into graves, rubble
like barney. the stone age.
headstones for Keisha
& Dantrell Davis. Girl X
marks the spot Candyman
minstreled celluloid screams
in the throats of white america.
an abacus of broken promises.
an aberration too close to gold
coasts. wires wild like snakes. snakes
like banks with redevelopment monies.
HOPE grants. good times filmed here.

& no good times filmed here.
fear of a nation & feeding
frenzies on the carcass. the bare
skeletal dreams of public
housing returning to earth.
dust. ghost. memory. maybe
raise three-bedroom townhomes.
the old grocery store where milk
& lottery tickets sold/bought
sandwiched between
young professionals like wonderbread.
cost an arm & leg leg arm head.
no g-d here, unless the church worship
the dollar.
the irony.
the green.

Ida B. Wells Testifies in the Ghost Town

1995–2011[13] in the rubble of the Ida B. Wells Homes

this is not the white city,
though perhaps it is a city
for whites. these are the Southern
Horrors: abandoned streets, boarded
buildings, empty tumbleweed lots.
you can hear Lake Michigan
in a coke can. this barren land
where children once moved
from these blocks to prison
auctioned.

blocks never been safe.

this a Red Record of displacement.
what happens when culture amnesias.
I sat on a train seventy years before
Montgomery. what'll this land be named:
scrapped plan for poor & Black, will it
be Lynchburg or Prisonton, New Laborville
the white city, again. these homes
had my name on them. now

I stand on rhodes near bridgeport,
astonished. prime land, my body, real
estate for the taking. dismembered
by hands the shade of ghost. my body
disfigured, again, this is what happens
when culture amnesias, when cities cancel
its promise, call it renewal. what happens
to those blue light monitored & standardized
test tracked, those forced into obsolete industrial
training, railroaded into new slave labor, orange
suited & disenfranchised, what do we do
with the forgotten, those left   out
to
hang
like ghosts.

I witness until the world does
until ghost stories are documented
& irrefutable, until America is haunted
by the spirits of those it says never happened.

How to Teach Poetry
in Chicago Public Schools
back to school, 1996

look clean. fresh
kicks, cut, jeans. iron
them shits. cuz even in uniform
the baddest student swagger on a 100
& those the kids you hope to build
with. the ones who got a crate
of albums on heart:
Weezy, Gucci, Waka Flocka
some may even have they own
bars for days. spit
alone in their room,
to their girl, a little
brother. they might
be reluctant to share
especially with a teacher
especially with a whiteboy.

start with a rhyme, something
quick. a half note behind
Westside double time.
their ears piqued, able
to roll with all those syllables.
now read a poem. something
slow, familial, familiar
an offering to Gwendolyn Brooks
& Carl Sandburg sitting on your shoulder.

ask where their favorite rapper is from:
J from Marcy
Ye, the South Side
everybody know Wayne
katrina's soldier boy.
from '97 to '03
have a firm, well-reasoned opinion
on who is better: Pac or Big.
after that Young Money, new language
Kanye couplets on memory.

photocopy Willie Perdomo's *Where I'm From*
the wrong way. do this to mess with them
to throw a monkey wrench into normal.
none of us are from Spanish Harlem.
but Englewood know bout police.
every block in the hundreds
got old men who talk shit
guns that fire cracker
grandmothers who stir
big pots. the whole West Side is
littered with nieces telling you
to look past bluebox street lights
cuz regardless of where you from
you from there, you know there
& have never been asked
to expert.

so speak on it.
talk about it.
all you gotta do
is sit that ass down
& write.

Lenard Clark Pedals for Air

March 21, 1997

on the first day of spring
weather might warm
long enough for kids to come outside
again, a miracle in a city where winter
can linger til may.

basketballs & bicycles in need of air
after sitting six months without
bounce & pedal.

in Bronzeville, home of the Black
renaissance, the South Side Community
Art Center, where Ms. Brooks & Margaret Burroughs
meet for tea, Black people have to pay 25 cents for air.

in Bridgeport, home of irish, polish & italian immigrants,
Chicago's mafia & the mayors daley, white folks
get all the air they wish for nothin.

from the windows of the Stateway Gardens
looking west across 12 lanes of the dan ryan express way
where eminent domain is another name for land grab
& colonization, Bridgeport is visible from Bronzeville.

& Lenard Clark didn't want to pay for what should be free
so he pedaled over the expressway & under the bridge & viaduct
into a neighborhood where white boys have been bragging
about keeping Blacks out since 1919.

& Frank Caruso Jr., the son of a guy
in the Chicago mob & two of his classmates
at De La Salle—the all-boys catholic school
of irish mayors & the italian outfit
(& if you think this is the first & last
time the two worked together i got
ocean front property in Cicero
i'd like to sell ya)—these older boys

saw Lenard peddling across borders
& chased the 13-year-old into an alley
& kicked his head into a coma.

this is how Black boys are bar-mitzvahed
in Chicago/america, by boot & brick, his boy
hood/body left deflated   in the alley
so far away   from home.

Baby Come On: An Ode to Footwork
1997

this is tap gone gangster.
in Wolof the Senegalese say dzugu:
to live wickedly. Juke is wicked music
unsanctioned house. a hundred & sixty beats
per minute.
                              here
folk move. turn the foot
Road Runner & Michael Jackson.
uprock on amphetamine. dance
in the war zone. in the war on drugs
Jack your body became run for your life
in place. on house arrest. take this space
small & make the most of it. glide
then magic, majestic, jack-knife leg
polyrhythm. pirouette stomp.
marionette legs on hot coals
on hot blocks. running man
in a circle or line / up. opposite
of prison. a battle no one gets hurt
most of the time. tip-toe kung-fu   kick
then drag the foot in molasses.
it's all that. all those hidden   Black
magic diasporic movements that might   kill whitefolk:
The Jig & Cakewalk   Pigeon Wing & Ring Dance
       & Capoeira in praise of Shango or DJ Rashad or
              R.P. Boo   or some other deity
          that don't look like a private dick or dick daley.

the foot is furious. the foot is working /   the foot is kicking   that ass
Black on Black time & space travel   sound   barrier   /
      broke
not confined to the speed   /   of the body.
       over   lo-fi low-budget bass   K-town favela funk   /.
       fuck
frenzy. fake out.   ghetto house. James Brown   jumping   bullets.
a ballet of the hustle. no money   no problem.
in the south they spoke Gullah   /   a creole

called it joog,   juke: something disorderly   / not   normal.
the foot   /   body not supposed to move   /   like
    that
not that rubber   band   /   not that   unshackled

        to gravity
                                              /   not that   free

A Moratorium on the Death Penalty

January 31, 2000

      today is a victory   for the hundreds
who persevered
who pushed the impossible
who fundraised in cafeterias
      in church community rooms
      with paper plates & mac & cheese
      made by mothers of sons facing state execution
who believe in Jesus's proclivity to save.
      it took a few journalists
who trust in long hours & interviews
whose reports bloomed above the muck
      & tabloid like lotus.
      law professors at Northwestern
who had an inclination & a class
      of committed students
who sifted thru thousands of documents
who uncovered truths the city hid
who shed new light. A People's Law Office
who filed & pro-bono-ed & argued on behalf of men
who Chicago tortured into confession before guantánamo
      a dark room, a simulated death & electric shocks
      on the watch & under the eye of states attorney richard m. daley
who never investigated or testified to what he knew
who rahm saved before subpoena.

      today is a victory   for the activists
who spend their lives ensuring the lives of others
      will not be taken by a racist state of injustice,
who are prison abolitionists & radical nuns
who are cultural organizers & writers & socialists
who are sisters & mothers & grandmothers
      of the incarcerated

      today is a monument to the moment
      the Death Row 10
      found each other inside
      a rotting system, men

who traded notes & formed a community
        a minyan, a cipher, a crew of support
who fought & wrote prayers in a bottle
who used the prison library
who read & decoded the legalese
who reached out & organized the outside
        from within
who made collage flyers to pass thru prison bars
who communicated & galvanized a movement
        10 to stir the masses
who will become thousands
who stand in for millions
        this city/country has murdered
        & stolen from their homes in the night
        thru decades of police torture & forced confessions
        the justice system blind to its own   white
                                                   supremacy.

        10 men
who in the bowels of county & state max security
        would tell what happened
whose words will rise thru letter
        & recording & shake the governor's mansion
who today declared a moratorium on death
        (maybe to save his own ass & reputation)
                                                but

        today is a monument
        that will lead to a ban
        to exonerations
        to reparations
        a path for the city/
        country to follow

Praise the House Party

May 17, 2000[14]

after Krista Franklin & Britteney Kapri

praise parents asleep in front of a television after a double or grinding the night of a third shift. *praise* the train i learned to ride: the red to the blue to a bus in the hopes the address was written down right on the quarter-sheet someone photocopied well before there ever was a kinko's. *praise* the desire to sneak out & listen to teenage DJs mash bits of records together that didn't make sense to the ear, new arrangements that propelled us out the house like an odd sonic bat signal so we could grind & jack the body & its parts. *praise* the body & its parts. *praise* the sweat & funk the body makes. *praise* the basement so hot it made the outfit you spent an hour preparing optional. *praise* new shoelaces & an old toothbrush to resurrect your busted kicks. *praise* jean shorts, the shortest ones. *praise* the wop & roger rabbit. *praise* radio shack & the mess of wires jammed into odd-fitting speakers. *praise* the vocational-high-school-know-how-to-rig bass box sub-woofers. *praise* Black hands manipulating black wax. *praise* the pans & knobs & casio keyboards put to use in ways manufacturers never imagined. *praise* the punch that wasn't spiked. *praise* the punch that was. *praise* counterfeit chemists & quarter-juice shamans. *praise* the folk who came to get you when you needed them to. *praise* the lock pick, the lookout, the abandoned loft, the house of squatters. *praise* the friend that told a friend. *praise* the heat between bodies making winter bearable. *praise* the night that becomes day. *praise* the get down, the packed jam. *praise* your mans, an employee with keys to the storage facility. *praise* the factories that shipped jobs elsewhere & the jobs that did stay. *praise* the empty spaces we filled with some old records & new styles & ourselves. *praise* ourselves for passing time, for keeping time & making time stop & making time irrelevant, for forgetting time other than a curfew, when you knew your moms would wake. *praise* your moms waking up & for getting down, back in bed, before she did.

Día de las Madres
May 13, 2001

after they sang "Las Mañanitas" in church
after King David whispered to his beloved
Dawn. after the children gave recuerdos
to their mothers & the husbands rushed
to 26th Street to get last-minute roses, after
all the tamales & elotes & champurrados
were laid out on the nice tablecloth
eaten one last time this sweet sunup,
fourteen abuelitas y madres walked
into an open field at 31st & Kostner
in La Villita/Little Village, South
Lawndale on the West Side & started
a hunger strike on mothers day.
they sought from the city what the city
promised: a school on par with white ones
in white neighborhoods where white kids
learn. the mothers want the same, want
what's fair, want Chicago/america
to treat their hijos with dignity & equity   too.

the field was so big you could forget you were
in the city. for nineteen days there was no food.
tents & chairs, wooded tables & song. art made
under the prairie sky. poems & music left at the feet
of the fourteen who suffered for the future,
who starved for honor long enough to win
honors classes, long enough for the school
to be named Social Justice. proof goliath's weak
his name daley & vallas & the blueprint
for privatized corporate education could
topple from the empty stomachs
of women in solidarity.

dawn has come.
rise up, my darling
sunlight is here

the mothers have won.

Kanye Says What's on Everybody's Mind

September 2, 2005

yo—i'm going to ad-lib a little bit.
Kanye West to Mike Myers

live from 30rock, the Roc boy
in the building tonight. late
registration just dropped. before
waves & tidals stormed the beach
before levees broke, before
the media wd say Black folk
loot & white folk survive.

hands stuck in luxe khakis.
rugby top & gold cross
across the neck. he went off
the top
   of the (astro)dome
freestyled, visibly shook
at the federal response
to Black death.
   ain't no such thing
as halfway crooks. news
bias, his own implication
lack of action, rambling
as waves crash
     in the mind
trying to translate rage
into language, to latch
onto & float. he rescued
ten syllables, a concise
editor of 16s, un-teleprompted
the words typed in his heart...

& Donda had done her job.
lullabied the legacy in her son's ear.
a Chicago State doctor channeling

her colleagues Gwendolyn Brooks
& Haki Madhubuti. their cultural son
storming live tv to tell the planet
what it can't wash over.

I Wasn't in Grant Park when obama Was Elected

November 4, 2008

i was on the ave, listening to the only democracy
i believe in. the longest-running youth open mic
in america. i was listening to the young
& the working, Black & unemployed
& Queer & radical imaginations dreaming
narrating the city/country they see
& fear. we were in a room of a hundred.
the street-lamps of milwaukee ave, our spot
light & faithful ear.

                    downtown
the pageantry projected to the planet
protected by guns & cpd. a Chicago
transplant invoked the dreams
of the founding fathers, not their captives
nor workers. the crowd screamed
droned the chant *yes we can.*

                    we were on the ave
laughing   cuz we don't believe you,
you need more people or different ones. we were
not taken with a president-elect, a united states
senator who stood for war abroad & in the streets
those here tonight have left to be free of, for a few
& devise strategies on how to build the block back
up, for real, not waiting for a trickle down or excuses
bout how a bill becomes a law, we watched school
house rock motherfucker & stay rocking the school
in the city of house & Big Bill Haywood.
our Black presidents are killed & rounded
into prison every day.

i wasn't in grant park when obama was elected
celebrating how great the country is. i was scheming
on the ave, with the people, cooking up a new one.

Republic Windows Workers Sit In
December 5, 2008

*I would like to encourage anyone who has been in a situation like us that they fight
and they demand their rights. They have nothing to lose.*
**Armando Robles, organizer of the Republic Windows
and Doors workers**

organizing began with whispers
in the break room. a tavern
after punch clock.

when the company comes to close
the workers will not leave. for six
days capitalism got its ass kicked.
the workers united will never be
defeated. they refuse to be refuse.
bossman could care less. they sit
like Buddhas, bodies on the line
in lawn chairs with coolers & hot
aluminum wrapped tamales.

the company thought they slick.
opened a non-unionized shop
in Red Oak, Iowa, under the name
echo. & the poems write themselves:
echoes of the Republic for which it stands.
the workers sit. the workers are the best
poets. five years from now will take over
the whole joint, fire the ceo
rename the company: New Era
build a worker-owned co-op
on this day, capitalism lost.

The Night the Modern Wing Was Bombed
February 22, 2010

a 44-foot mural on a 50-foot wall in 14 minutes
during a blizzard at 3 in the morning. caught
security, cpd, the whole city, yawning
slippin, sleeping. writers plottin, creepin
geared up: night vision, fat caps, krylon
in knapsacks, backpacks, bandanna face masks.
fame seekin, names flying in night, not white
game tweakin. limestone brick wall, spray that
new modern wing, dumb loot, schools closed
art cut, this the place that / nothing new. 18 bucks
on public land impossible for the public view.
outside where the public view, outside
where the public do. the anonymous wrote
Modern Art above the student entrance
free class, public school. Made U Look
clean ass / hand style, this ain't /no other crew.
the news peeped game, internets, blogs too.
the museum in they feelings, don't want discourse
bout what the arts will do or what artists do
or why so few Chicagoans hang in the museum
why only dead white motherfuckers on the wall
so few painters of Color, who painting with color
bang the mausoleum / why it cost so much
why the art sucks / why they keep art
for the few, away from the many
modern art bandits / pulled off
the heist of the century. after the statute
of limitations / come get me / we gon build
a statue without limits, wave a W
flag & burn an L in the entry.

When King Louie First Heard the Word *Chiraq*
Summer 2010

it was so hot
freezers became   furnaces.
               all the cheese
     melted from spicy chips.
     eveybody's hands were red.
the air
     a sleeping bag
of blood.
     shoes dangled on telephone wires
 like missiles
     toes
tigers. pick one
block everybody
know somebody
who not
a body
anymore.
       King Louie
must've been coming out the bag
of a crown royal, purple velour wrapped
round his hand, bands, knots, a split
swisher, sweet about his mane of wool.
eyes a flame, feet dipped in Bronze
nikes like the ville, the fire. this time

a kid might've said it slick.
someone's lil cousin making
a geopolitical assessment,
a vernacular ingenious flip
addressing the amount
of violence & occupying forces
responsible for the bodies
& militarization of the block,
for food deserts & desert eagles,
a critical pronouncement
countering the myth
of intervention & the war

on drugs, some little body
                    dropped
                         this Chiraq
out the mouth
like a screwdriver,
running from forces
better funded & more
insidious & sadistic.

          & King Louie
mighta waited for the block
to clear, for the heat to dissipate
like october, the lights to chill
til dusk, as this shiny gem
laid in the street like someone
          lost a dead
president but didn't know it.
he scooped it in his pocket.
touched its smooth Black earth
like obsidian, this history & death
he held close, anticipating the right
moment to share, to say it like a spell,
a whisper he plucked from air & was keeping
for the fall
to come

An Elegy for Dr. Margaret Burroughs
November 22, 2010

if you did not etch metal into Black ink
if you did not travel to learn with the Mexican muralists
if you & Charlie did not think African history
       important to re/member & re/present in Black light
       Black thought, Black ideas in Black minds
       in Black brains
if you did not build an institution in your house & basement
if you did not have a door don l. lee could open
       cuz he needed someone   to talk to
if you were not here, Black Arts wouldn't have been
       mothered in this city. the wall of respect
       wouldn't have risen & burned
       in the imagination of the South Side
if you were not here, no AfriCOBRA
       no South Side Community Arts Center
       no institutions, no memory & images
       of girls at their birthday or portraits
       of Du Bois & Malcolm & heroes
       whi-te cubes wouldn't hold
if you were not here, no honest portrayal of Beauty
       nothing authentic, no celebration
       of African forms
if you & Ms. Brooks were not
       classmates & sisters:
       no OBAC
       no Carolyn Rodgers
       no Angela Jackson
       no Walter Bradford
if you were not here, no Black language
       no Black poetic, no ritual song
       in this segregated Chicago

the lineage is you
& Ms. Brooks
& Haki
& hip-hop
& ALL
pro-Black centered words

which is to say true
words for once that stay
telling it how it is.
ALL the voices needed
you nurtured

if you were not here,
       ALL those words & images
       ALL those pro-Black celebratory songs
       ALL the poets you mother tongued,
       ALL the painters' hands you poured kool-aid colors in
if you were not here, generations of american artists would not be.
       you rescued us from english class
       you took some off the block, posted on the corner
       you told us to dream & imagine & build
            our legacies on the shoulders of those before
       you made us believe Art is a language people need

you lived among the people
Bronzeville whirling & warping your doorstep
       a mess of family & pigeons
       a house full of gems & germs
you were always doing your job
       getting our minds right
       telling the next generation (& the generation after &
       after that)
       to be about something, this is what you left

& you left so much
& you will always be
& you will always be   here
in a purple caftan & headdress
in acid mikes with no socks on
       you stayed fresh like that
& you left Us the desire to be fresh
to make & tell
& re/tell
& re/make
& re/main
& re/member
& re/present

always
          here, you are
the heart   of the story/city
in order to re/member ourselves
we must   speak
your name

A Dedication to the Inaugural Poet

May 16, 2011 *for Ms. Chanel Sosa*

after reading at the mayor's inauguration
the poet is unimpressed. backstage
w/ secret service & bureaucratic aides
she is on the phone texting her boo
who is twenty w/ three kids & three baby
mamas. a light-skinned GD
w/ green eyes. she is eighteen. Black
Dominican y Colombian w/ an accent
everyone loves. she's an alternative
high school senior who got her hair did
on the West Side the day before; streaks
of some electric moon & spiked bangs.
her mother is not here. nor her siblings.
the last time she saw her father, he told her
he would kill her.
               in the procession line
after the ceremony, the poet waits
to be taken to city hall to stand
with multi-hued children the mayor
photo-ops in front of. vice-president
joe biden grabs her hand, says he really felt her
poem (you can see in the video joe's real).
the new old mayor daley brushes by
without a word. gets stuck in the traffic of dark
suits & backs into the poet as if she's not there.
he's posing with the 9-year-old white girl who played
america the beautiful on violin.

the poet is big & grown & not cute
on stage. she is beautiful tributing the river
she swims: Brooks & Sandburg, invoking
Algren & Etta James, a realist blues, the most
honest utterance this day.

the poet is undaunted in the line of aldermen.
unmoved by the mayor's wife's congratulations.

she knows she was asked here to be a flower arrangement.
she knows some lines have been redacted
        by press secretaries & homeland security.
she knows backstage she was just another Black girl
        the archbishop didn't say hello to.
she knows in an hour she will take the red line
        back to Chatham where there is not a grocery store
        or millennium park, where there has not been a new day
        in any of her eighteen years.

she will take the train all the way south
where politicians' promises don't reach.

at the end of this day
she is still poor & working
even if she's heading to college
her family will be, her community,
the young men she loves, who she calls
shadows, will remain, without
any of what the mayor's children have.

Memoir of the Red X

June 27, 2012[15]

after Hebru Brantley

> *When I see the blood, I will pass over you, and the plague shall not be upon you to destroy you, when I smite the land of Egypt.*
> **Exodus 12:13**

blood on the door.
red slashes in a white box.
a warning what lurks.
a warring. a target.
an invitation to squat.
a pyre to blaze. a death
knell for neighborhoods
south, west. marks the spot
families were, industry was.
illiterate's autograph.
mark of danger. great
migration dream catcher.
promise breaker. temporary
detention center before
land grab. body count.
connotes new orleans
homes, haunted. ghosts
here. Malcolm's memorial.
a red cross inverted
perverted. an emergency
no one scrambles to fix.

Chief Keef's Epiphany at Lollapalooza

August 4, 2012

from stage
he can see
thousands
crowd surf
in a gated
Grant Park.
land stolen
by those
who mosh pit.

his whole camp
faces the Great
Lake: eyes on
the prize
on water, some
have never seen.

heat rises
from the ground
like fire in the brush
in the streets.

thousands of hands,
bodies bounce around
mouth every word

pink mouths
around every word

pink mouths
around every n-word.

more shit
he don't
like

Teachers' Strike in the Chicago Tradition
September 10, 2012

The assault on public education started here. It needs to end here.
Karen Lewis, CTU president

the teachers march in Chicago.
red in the streets again, perpetually.
this is a union town, after all
Most radical of American cities:[16]
Nelson Algren would say

this a fight against a mayor
who sold the unions out
to nafta & the clinton white house.

the teachers' strike
in the Chicago tradition
allied with trade unionists
& Pullman porters. in solidarity
with the Haymarket martyrs
& Republic Windows workers.

the teachers honor those who died
in the 1937 memorial day massacre
when cops shot steelworkers.
they honor those who build & built
the country, who ensured the eight-hour day.

in the name of:
Lucy Parsons
Albert Parsons
& Rudy Lozano

in the name of:
Gene Debs
Mother Jones
Addie Wyatt
Jane Addams &
The Pullman Porters

in the name of Studs Terkel
& his red socks
in solidarity, he rocks from the grave
& would've been on the picket line
today, with the teachers
in the long haul
standing with the many
standing with the teachers
firmly rooted in the Chicago tradition:
on the shoulders of giants
who knocked down goliath
fighting the good fight
for the future of All

During Ramadan the Gates of Heaven Are Open

July 14, 2013[17]

the day after not guilty
a sunday, during Ramadan
a town hall for young people
deliberately marginalized.
they assert themselves at the center
of public discourse. of course
where they belong, have always
been. the wooden stage
painted Black in a second-floor
loft overlooking Milwaukee Avenue
& Division Street.

two Muslim women
take the stage. one
after the other. one
in a headscarf. one
not.
           Ashley
survived the foster-care system
was adopted by a hip-hop mother
in Uptown & kinda looks white
but who knows, really. she converted
to Islam in high school. a super volunteer
at IMAN, the Inner-City Muslim Action Network.
she was unsure what to say
but decided to speak
from the heart. when she heard
the verdict she cried & dry heaved
cuz there was nothing inside to throw up.
she is weeping now, telling a room
of young people, who gathered here
cuz they had nowhere else to go,
during Ramadan the gates of heaven
are open. she is fasting & disciplined
like the work & organizing needs to be.

Farwa is Pakistani
in all-Black everything.

she too did not want to speak
but was moved to do so.
this young woman who weeps
open & often, a chronic lament
          & heartache,
is poised today. mourning
in crisis, righteous
she is
moved to tell the story of Ashura,
a day of fasting & rage
where a community does not say *salaam.*
there is no peace today
it is ok
to rage today
to pray today
for patience.

these two women
american *muezzin*
young & brave
& calling us to *adhan*
to *salat*, to pray
where we gather:

Allahu Akbar!
in the name of Emmett Till
in the name of Trayvon Martin
Allahu Akbar!
in the name of Rekia Boyd
in the name of Oscar Grant
Allahu Akbar!
in the name of Fred Hampton
in the name of the many names we cannot name
Allahu Akbar!
Allahu Akbar!

Ms. Devine Explains the Meaning of Modern Art: A Found Poem

Spring 2014

Veteran Art Institute security guard Cookie Devine in the Christopher Williams
exhibition at the Art Institute of Chicago regarding the Bouquet for Jan Ader and
Christopher D'Arcangelo.

at first i didn't know what it was. just a room with a picture in it. but today a high school group come in & i'm at the other end & gettin worried
like i'ma haveta quiet them cuz you know, they rustlin. but once they
come past the wall & see this empty room & the lights is dark, they turn
back & see there's a picture of flowers on the wall, just one picture, so
it mus mean somethin. the students, well they get to quiet. it jus trans-
forms them like they at a funeral or somethin. they shoulders go slack,
heads drop in remorse, they rememberin.

i heard one lady say, one of my co-workers, i can't remember exactly
what she say but she say, while we passin on shifts, that the flowers are
for friends of his who died real young. well this is my opinion, but in
Chicago we know what that is. so when kids come into this room & it's
uncluttered like a funeral parlor it's supposed to mean the time & space
you need to mourn. the white & little light in here is supposed to mean
you can think different bout the person who not here anymore. the flowers in that picture is supposed to mean something beautiful, some kind
of memory that's there but'll fade away, like the flowers will.

& the students in that room are dead quiet, like they prayin or somethin.
i seen it happen. they might not know the artist's name or whatever but
they feel what's going on, cuz they goin thru it theyself. they all lost
somebody & in my opinion that's somethin, they can respect.

Two Cities Celebrate Independence Day

July 4–7, 2014[18]

1

midwest weekenders
gather at the lakefront.
blue eyes over navy pier.

the breeze has ease,
distant lite jazz. a cacophony
of calm & citronella.

the sky on fire above
the mighty Michigan
boasts. penthouses,

sailboats stock sun–
burnt faces alight in laughter
& lite beer. a lightness

here. a whiteness.
a luxury to hear blasts
& not flinch or think

someone you love is not.
here is not a land of blood
or body. all remains, remain

well. deposit box inheritance.
the future a right. bright. awash
in light. the holiday is every

day

neighborhoods will bloom tonight.

mini-arsenals stockpiled from Indiana.
smoke & fire in the streets & alleys.
corner boys & working fathers make
the sky burn. the light on the block
warms the faces of little ones, mothers
on stoops finally sitting for a moment
to watch dusk turn the color of candy.

bustelo cans are cannons. roman candles
in county men's hands launch fireballs
into the dark, raging against the stars.

downtown the 1812 overture will whisper
gently over the water. but here quarter sticks
of dynamite bass drum a requiem for the fire
crackers take & for those who won't make it

tonight:

Warren Robison, 16, will be shot 20
times by police with his hands in the air.

tonight

Pedro Rios, 14, will run like a boy
until the cops fire two in his back.

small armies overrun the streets.
free & aimless, makeshift orchestras
of whistles, bottles, bombs. the war
of each day, reenacted every

night.

We Charge Genocide

November 13, 2014

...the Chicago Police Department is in violation of Articles 2, 10, 11, 12, 13 and 14 of the Convention of Torture, through the cruel, inhuman, and degrading treatment of youth of color in Chicago.

We Charge Genocide UN Shadow Report

in front of the world eight
Black, Brown, Queer young folk
rock braids & locs & matching t-shirts
that read: *The Chicago Police Dept. Killed
Dominique Franklin* like they did Fred.
in the hall of the United Nations
for half an hour leaning into each other
heads bent in prayer & power calling to Damo,
their homie, tasered while handcuffed
outside a Walgreens with some candy
or toothpaste in his pocket & who is now
no more. this for those who are no more.
for 30 minutes in silence, hands clasped to fists
raised to heaven like John Carlos & Tommie Smith,
the time Rekia Boyd laid in the street
after an off-duty cop shot her in the head.
again & always there is Black death & today
it receives its proper name, its one true
name. Chicago youth stand on the world
stage to mourn & proclaim. to pronounce
formally, finally, in no uncertain terms:

Atoning for the Neoliberal in All
or rahm emanuel as the Chicken on Kapparot
written on the eve & day of Yom Kippur, September 22–23, 2015

*Do you call that a fast, a day when the Lord is favorable? No, this is the fast I desire: To
unlock the fetters of wickedness, and untie the cords of the yoke, to let the oppressed go free.*
Isaiah 58: 5-6

you are the first jewish mayor of Chicago
but have not lit one yahrzeit candle
for people murdered by the police.

you vacation in montana with the governor,
bring your family to Chile on a whim
& never worry about crossing borders
or encountering their patrolmen
or the rent upon return.

your grandparents sought refuge here.
escaping those trying to end them.
they came, worked, learned, created
a life that enabled your parents to raise you
in the suburbs: the immigrant face of the american dream.

you dismantle the same system from which your family benefited:
union pay, livable wages, park space safe enough to play outside
arts funding to take ballet, a decent well-rounded public education.

the same ladder your family climbed
you kick the rungs from.

if the schools, housing, health care
trauma centers & corners that cause trauma
are fair across this flat, segregated land—
then eat today. every day there is a harvest
on the carcass of the city for sale. the satiated
carve at a distance, plan, map & redistrict
with careless indifference. how many times
have you been to Kenwood, Woodlawn
North Lawndale. what are the names of the people
you know there. what homes have you sat in.

how can you fast
this week, when food
was refused by grandmothers
& educators & organizers
in your backyard, in the front
lawn of a school Chief Keef attended
in a neighborhood you militarize;
more guns & police your solution
to poverty or an extermination strategy.

how can you fast
when you couldn't stand
in the same room with
those on hunger strike.
in a public forum
you don't listen.
you are the antithetical
Studs Terkel

this is not the city he loved
to listen to, not the city
your grandparents were promised

where is your apology
for sending so many jobs elsewhere
for privileging your children's future
& pillaging others'

what do you know of labor
& no savings account & counting
pennies for a pass, for permission to move
or see a movie or museum in this city
of no access & grand canyons of inequity.

your middle name is Israel
it's come to mean apartheid
in the city, you are mayor
& in Palestine, the city
your family colonized.

there is no safety
        said my G-d
for the wicked[19]

for the divvier of cities
for the divider of nations
for the ignorer of horror
for the builder of walls

atone for the smug assuredness
atone for the maintenance of two cities
        stratified & unrecognizable to the other
atone for the bounty of the north side
        the scarcity of the south
        the want of the west
atone for the erasure of the public
        school, space, housing, parking
atone for the centrism, the move right
        the kowtow to corporations
atone for the inconceivable income disparity
        between those funding your campaign
        & those over whom you reign
atone for the city's change
        its whitewash & removable
        workers who used to make it
        work by working
        in jobs with pensions
        & benefits
atone for the benefits we have
        by merely being white
        on the north side of the city
        country where that is enough
        to make you safe & not think
        about driving a car or going
        for a jog or walk outside
atone for the rite to the city
        that's for some, not for all
        not for real

israel means may G-d prevail
& we pray that's real, for real

                              amen

400 Days

October 20, 2014–November 24, 2015
after Nazim Hikmet

in 400 days
        i've gone thru 3 journals
worked
        on 2 books, a play & a movie
                about house music.
i left a lover
        & found another.
lost 2 teeth
        got 4 stitches, broke
                a finger in a fight
& sat in the barber shop for 24 fades
        mostly from Rob at Chicago's Best
except when i'm traveling & i've learned
not to get a haircut while traveling.

        i've had students graduate
grow hair on their face, had sex
for the 1st time. some are starting
        college, a few have
                        been shot:
1 thru the lung
                he lived, made a mix tape.
1 in a parked car
        waiting to see his son
who will now have to wait
                        forever.
the city has opened   .
                hundreds
of new restaurants, private social clubs
                closed public schools
put on a halloween parade
        an irish day parade
        a columbus day parade
        a new year's celebration
                erected condos
        targets
                & never once

                              apologized.
there have been thousands
                    of masterpieces
              artists painted
                    on the streets
for the people. but
              the city removed
                    cuz art is racialized
                         & the city
              thinks some artists
                              criminal.
i started
              eating chicken again
in the last 400 days, the doctor said
                    less sugar.
the city is chicken
                    to apologize
              & will never say anything sweet.
the city makes Black
              a target. a video game
a city of zombies, the walking dead.
                    for 400 days cpd, the state's attorney
the mayor's office hid evidence
              tape, bullets
              & didn't apologize
              for any of it.
400 days ago
              toddlers were not
yet & now cry thru the night.
              they see a city
of ghosts. walking
              Laquan, the other
way, still shot
              16 times.
no life
              in the eyes
of cops, anita. mayor rahm
looks dead
              into the camera
                    & lies
              for 400 days

                    the cubs threatened
        victory
                        but justice
            will have to wait
til next year

The Night the Cubs Win the World Series
November 2, 2016

my pops chariots a drunken lady
home safely. they pull to the side
of the road in the dark of West Irving
Park & listen to one out, then two, then
weep at the blast of the improbable
come.

i too have tears when talking
to him finally. he is in the melee
of the night trying to celebrate, trying
to hustle the loot for whatever number
mortgage he's on, before the banks pounce
like Kris Bryant on a grounder & throw him out.

we imagine this is for all the fathers
weeping, the mothers' names that chalk
the wall, the grandparents who couldn't
be here. the generations who loved
without hardware, but this is
the arrogance of the north side
incarnate. the double play, double
standard turned over like property.

The Cubs did not win the World Series
tonight. a game in north america maybe
the nation's pastime. but the curse is
not lifted in the shadow of the bloodiest
weekend of the year
                                    though the north side
celebrates its constant win. its distance
from the south & west. a delight, a dream
team that's not, but reads so white,
a side so white, they're dumping beer
on each other's heads to metaphor
the excess. what world are we celebrating.

all week long the minstreled indian
smiles from the arm of the Cleveland

hitters as Natives are mauled by dogs
& gas in Cannon Ball, North Dakota
defending their home base & water supply.

the mayor keeps popping up
on camera smiling like a jackass.
the owner upholds the trophy
in the club house & writes checks
to the campaigns of fascists
in the mist of champagne.

the blue flag flying the W
stands for whiteness & blue lives.

i can't celebrate the one side
or one story. not for a single
night or 108 years or 180.

i can't cheer for this
national pastime
of curses fixed
for generations;
redlined, red blooded
american & perennial.

Chicago Has My Heart

March 4, 2017

don't ask me to leave
don't force me to go
when the coasts call
when the rents rise
when the city i know
is unrecognizable.
it's mine, not alone
not to own.

Chicago has my heart
at the lake, on the train
in the first days of spring
that remind us why we live
here, at all, have bodies
can use them outside the cold
restrictions of clothing, the confines
of neighborhood.

Chicago has my heart
the land i'm most confident:
give me an address, i'll get us
there. i know the grid, blocks
got people in these streets
students whose family
run the breakfast spot
on 79th near Haki
who is still here
building temples
to Black lives, monuments
to Mama Gwendolyn

my family is here. my father,
six blocks from me in Albany Park,
the mayor of the city's broke dreams
he holds them in his growing belly
his breaking heart, falling
asleep in front of the television
chatting thru the night in his taxi

the city with money calls an uber,
he drives new residents to wherever
they wish to go. thank G-d
for the hustle, the hustler, my father
the kindest, most incompetent
businessman here. he doesn't
swindle or cheat, he is honest
& fair, what a sucker
this city makes of sweet
men.
                    like me
i guess, i just
want justice
& someone
to read poems to
to u

Chicago, my heart
is all the people
who make it
who are making it
barely, in the 77 hoods.
i hate the viaducts
the millionaires
who urban plan them
from the suburbs
they resurrect
downtown

Chicago you have my heart
my whole history, my people
you saved, seeking refuge here
tucked in apartments in Ukrainian
Village & North Lawndale.
you saved them from history
while destroying others'.
my mother left. my brother
moved. my friends gone:
too much rent, debt
you killed some off
you are a ghost mound

i stalk, still, Chicago
you have my heart
split in two
like the city
& stories you tell
but i am one
not two
i am one
second will not do
you can't continue
to break us
in two, in remade
refurbished, renewed
models for the few.

Chicago has my heart
                but
my head
my hands
my body
with the people
who build
who have a limit
& can break
& tear
it down & stop it
from becoming
what it's becoming

what is it becoming

Chicago has my heart
                but
the hearts of those
who call this home
who root & champion
the losers & villains
who run this place
who put on for the shitty
pizza & arctic weather

we will turn our backs
on the very land we are
locked in, turn our backs
on the capital wage-slaves
you've made us become.
we will burn your memory
in effigy & house dance
in the afterglow

we rise, Chicago
this body
politic will rise
our fire will burn
again

Notes

1   X names of the Native signees: To-pen-e-bee, his x mark; Sau-ko-noek, his x mark; Che-che-bin-quay, his x mark; Joseph, his x mark; Wah-mix-i-co, his x mark; Ob-wa-qua-unk, his x mark; N-saw-way-quet, his x mark; Puk-quech-a-min-nee, his x mark; Nah-che-wine, his x mark; Ke-wase, his x mark; Wah-bou-seh, his x mark; Mang-e-sett, his x mark; Caw-we-saut, his x mark; Ah-be-te-ke-zhic, his x mark; Pat-e-go-shuc, his x mark; E-to-wow-cote, his x mark; Shim-e-nah, his x mark; O-chee-pwaise, his x mark; Ce-nah-ge-win, his x mark; Shaw-waw-nas-see, his x mark; Shab-eh-nay, his x mark; Mac-a-ta-o-shic, his x mark; Squah-ke-zic, his x mark; Mah-che-o-tah-way, his x mark; Cha-ke-te-ah, his x mark; Me-am-ese, his x mark, Shay-tee, his x mark; Kee-new, his x mark; Ne-bay-noc-scum, his x mark; Naw-bay-caw, his x mark; O'Kee-mase, his x mark; Saw-o-tup, his x mark; Me-tai-way, his x mark; Na-ma-ta-way-shuc, his x mark; Shaw-waw-nuk-wuk, his x mark; Nah-che-wah, his x mark; Sho-bon-nier, his x mark; Me-nuk-quet, his x mark; Chis-in-ke-bah, his x mark; Mix-e-maung, his x mark; Nah-bwait, his x mark; Sen-e-bau-um, his x mark; Puk-won, his x mark; Wa-be-no-say, his x mark; Mon-tou-ish, his x mark; No-nee, his x mark; Mas-quat, his x mark; Sho-min, his x mark; Ah-take, his x mark; He-me-nah-wah, his x mark; Che-pec-co-quah, his x mark; Mis-quab-o-no-quah, his x mark; Wah-be-Kai, his x mark; Ma-ca-ta-ke-shic, his x mark; Sho-min, his x mark; She-mah-gah, his x mark; O'ke-mah-wah-ba-see, his x mark; Na-mash, his x mark; Shab-y-a-tuk, his x mark; Ah-cah-o-mah, his x mark; Quah-quah, tah, his x mark; Ah-sag-a-mish-cum, his x mark; Pa-mob-a-mee, his x mark; Nay-o-say, his x mark; Ce-tah-quah, his x mark; Ce-ku-tay, his x mark; Sauk-ee, his x mark; Ah-quee-wee, his x mark; Ta-cau-ko, his x mark; Me-shim-e-nah, his x mark; Wah-sus-kuk, his x mark; Pe-nay-o-cat, his x mark; Paymaw-suc, his x mark; Pe-she-ka, his x mark; Shaw-we-mon-e-tay, his x mark; Ah-be-nab, his x mark; Sau-sau-quas-see, his x mark.

2   Opening of the Union Stockyard.

3   The last writings of Albert Parsons, published in the *Alarm*, November 5, 1887, a week before his execution.

4   Italics are phrases from Debs's speech upon his release from prison November 23, 1895, quoted in the *Chicago Chronicle* & Karl Marx's *Capital*.

5   A section of German criminal code that made homosexuality a crime from 1871 to 1994.

6   Founder of the political Latino street organization the Young Lords.

7   *Division Street: America* is published.

8   A line from Haki Madhubuti's poem "The Wall."

9   A line from Gwendolyn Brooks's poem "The Wall."

10   "The Hawk" refers to Chicago's cold wind. Used in the *Chicago Defender*, October 20, 1936, and famously in Lou Rawls's 1967 *Dead End Street*.

11   Language removed from the cityofchicago.org website.

12 The demolition of Cabrini Green housing begins.
13 Housing and Urban Development begins and ends demolition of the Ida B. Wells Homes in Bronzeville.
14 City Council passes a rave ordinance, a stricter enforcement of the juice-bar ordinance of April 1, 1987.
15 City Council passes an ordinance marking "dangerous buildings" with red Xs in order to warn first responders about "structural conditions" in "buildings that could create danger for crews responding to fires. These conditions include weak truss or other roofing systems, missing mortar, rotted or damaged timbers."
16 Big Bill Haywood was a socialist and one of the founders of the Industrial Workers of the World, started in Chicago in 1904.
17 The day after a Florida jury finds the murderer of Trayvon Martin not guilty.
18 Eight-two people were shot this weekend. Fourteen of them died.
19 Isaiah 57:21.

Illustration Credits

Illustrators:
Max Sansing
Troy Scat
Hebru Brantley
Paul Branton
Bianca Pastel
Runsy

1. Jean Baptiste Point duSable
illustration by by Max Sansing

2. Gwendolyn Brooks
illustration by Max Sansing

3. Lorraine Hansberry
illustration by Max Sansing

4. Muddy Waters
illustration by Troy Scat

5. Sun Ra
illustration by Hebru Brantley

6. Studs Terkel
illustration by Troy Scat

7. Fred Hampton
illustration by Paul Branton

8. Haki Madhubuti
illustration by Troy Scat

9. Ron Hardy
illustration by Bianca Pastel

10. Rudy Lozano
illustration by Runsy

11. Harold Washington
illustrated by Hebru Brantley

12. Common
illustrated by Paul Branton

13. Ida B. Wells-Barnett
illustrated by Bianca Pastel

14. The Mothers & Grandmothers
illustrated by Runsy

15. Kanye West
illustrated by Hebru Brantley

16. King Louie
illustrated by Runsy

17. Dr. Margaret Burroughs
illustrated by Paul Branton

18. Chief Keef
illustrated by Bianca Pastel

Acknowledgments

teamwork makes the dream work. i lean heavy on my community, my family forged in blood & fire. Moms, the fighter. Pops, the storyteller. Aunt Joyce, who has transitioned, my Chicago guide to the art hustle. she loved the city, its artists, put on for them & carved spaces for them to grind & shine. my Uncle Steve, the writer & historian, who loves NYC like i do this burg, a civic pride like Jane Jacobs. my brother Eric, the mensch & disciplined educator & father. my sister Elyse, the who manages to put up with my family with grace & light. Addison & Colin, niece & nephew, who are so different & hilarious & lovely & free. Cheryl & Sasha, y'all a badass, amazing duo.

Young Chicago Authors (YCA) is a home & house i built with the many who are there and who have left and who return. Rebecca Hunter, it would be impossible without your vision & dedication to the growth & integrity of this work. To the staff & team at YCA i am indebted to your belief in making the city anew, again, a more better & fresher space for all.

Louder Than A Bomb (LTAB) is a movement. And at this point there have been tens of thousands and more who have participated and made it so. If you care & believe young people, young artists can shape and shift and sing the world as it is & as it will be, this is a space for you to dream, too. This fountain of youth, of freshness & could-give-a-fuck-lessness & care the most, i rock with y'all too tough: the poets & coaches & teachers & volunteers & thousand partners & festival staff it takes to pull off the impossible, salutes.

a generous partner in this work makes this book, *A People's History of Chicago*, possible, The Lannan Foundation and the residency i was able to take in Marfa, texas, where this book really came together. I had a month of isolation, to think & read & write & edit & invest in this project. It was the first time in my life someone said this space is for you to make, that's it, no song & dance, no also teach fifty classes, just create, what a privilege & essential gift & honor.

in texas, i was writing essentially two books & Nate Marshall said to just focus on one. He is the editor, homie & partner in BreakBeats & LTAB/YCA scheming. The student has become the teacher & i am eternally grateful to learn from such an incredible poet & man.

Fatimah Ashgar put eyes on the script & clipped & made essential edits & suggestions & made it more & better. She is an artist with so many talents, who's also an incredible cheerleader, an encourager & champion in your corner.

Jamila Woods is Bonnie. My ride-or-die aesthetic thought partner. There is more music cuz of her syntactical suggestions & presence on the planet.

i wouldn't be alive if not for the brotherhood i share with Idris Goodwin, Hip-Hop's August Wilson. We shit-talked & dreamed a way to change the whole canon.

there are countless other comrades & brothers & sisters in this work. Adam Mansbach, Angel Nafis are two dumb talented & dumb people i love the most.

the folks at Haymarket Books are squad. Anthony Arnove & Julie Fain trust me to create & to have such high-quality brilliant people say yes to your work, your inner turned out, is a blessing. Jim Plank is as down as they come. Sarah Grey is nice af with the editorial eye. Thank you Nisha & Rachel & Caroline & the whole team who make this book & all these words possible.

the artists who blessed these poems with beautiful tributes & portraits i'm forever down for. Hebru Brantley is the homie & GOAT. His downness astounding. His team, Max Sansing, Troy Scat & Bianca Pastel are stupid talents whose work I love & look forward to seeing more & more of. Paul Branton is a true school head whose brush & pen tribute the city of hustlers. Runsy is a former student, whose style & talent have no ceilings.

my mentors are my guides: Bill Ayers & Bernardine Dorn, Rick Kogan, Haki Madhubuti. many informally, but these Chicago institutions have paved a way for me to walk in the world: gatherers of story & song & with a sense of fairness & justice that is unbreakable.

there is a crew around me that make *A People's History of Chicago* real. Brett Neiman has designed every one of my covers & is a renaissance man of the people. Mickayla Johnson, Tammy Job & Nick Ward are out here keeping me grinding & on time. Tara Mahadevan is spreading the word like bo$$ & is high-key the creative director of the whole project. It is a pleasure & honor to work with Ryan at Biz3. & there are many more i am sure i am forgetting & also they many to come. The plan to make this book utilitarian, a spoon or shank or lifeboat. I plan on doing at least 180 readings in 365 days & workshops surrounding the book to have many folk i interact with add their voices & stories to the narrative of this great & troubled city.

so i thank you, the reader, in advance, for holding it down & pushing us forward.

Also Available from Haymarket Books

Before the Next Bomb Drops: Rising Up from Brooklyn to Palestine
Remi Kenazi

L-Vis Lives: Racemusic Poems
Kevin Coval

Long Shot: The Triumphs and Struggles of an NBA Freedon Fighter
Craig Hodges with Rory Fanning, foreword by Dave Zirin

Lucy Parsons: An American Revolutionary
Carolyn Ashbaugh

Mayor 1%: Rahm Emanuel and the Rise of Chicago's 99%
Kari Lydersen

People Wasn't Made to Burn:
A True Story of Housing, Race, and Murder in Chicago
Joe Allen

Schtick: These Are the Poems, People
Kevin Coval

Whiskey of Our Discontent:
Gwendolyn Brooks as Conscience and Change Agent
Edited by Quraysh Ali Lansana and Georgia A. Popoff,
introduction by Sonia Sanchez

About Haymarket Books

Haymarket Books is a nonprofit, progressive book distributor and publisher, a project of the Center for Economic Research and Social Change. We believe that activists need to take ideas, history, and politics into the many struggles for social justice today. Learning the lessons of past victories, as well as defeats, can arm a new generation of fighters for a better world. As Karl Marx said, "The philosophers have merely interpreted the world; the point, however, is to change it."

We take inspiration and courage from our namesakes, the Haymarket Martyrs, who gave their lives fighting for a better world. Their 1886 struggle for the eight-hour day, which gave us May Day, the international workers' holiday, reminds workers around the world that ordinary people can organize and struggle for their own liberation. These struggles continue today across the globe—struggles against oppression, exploitation, hunger, and poverty.

It was August Spies, one of the Martyrs targeted for being an immigrant and an anarchist, who predicted the battles being fought to this day. "If you think that by hanging us you can stamp out the labor movement," Spies told the judge, "then hang us. Here you will tread upon a spark, but here, and there, and behind you, and in front of you, and everywhere, the flames will blaze up. It is a subterranean fire. You cannot put it out. The ground is on fire upon which you stand."

We could not succeed in our publishing efforts without the generous financial support of our readers. Many people contribute to our project through the Haymarket Sustainers program, where donors receive free books in return for their monetary support. If you would like to be a part of this program, please contact us at info@haymarketbooks.org.

Shop our full catalog online at www.haymarketbooks.org.

About the BreakBeat Poets Series

The BreakBeat Poets series, curated by Kevin Coval and Nate Marshall, is committed to work that brings the aesthetic of hip-hop practice to the page. These books are a cipher for the fresh, with an eye always to the next. We strive to center and showcase some of the most exciting voices in literature, art, and culture.

BreakBeat Poets Series titles include:

The BreakBeat Poets: New American Poetry in the Age of Hip-Hop, edited by Kevin Coval, Quraysh Ali Lansana, and Nate Marshall

This is Modern Art: A Play, Idris Goodwin and Kevin Coval

My Mother Was a Freedom Fighter, Aja Monet

Electric Arches, Eve Ewing (forthcoming)

Black Girl Magic, edited by Mahogany Browne, Jamila Woods, and Idrissa Simmonds (forthcoming)